Tastes of Tuscany

*Treasured Family
Recipes and Vignettes
from the
Heartland of Italy*

Tastes of Tuscany

Treasured Family
Recipes and Vignettes
from the
Heartland of Italy

Liana Giovannini Figone

Sincei Auguri!
Liana G. Figone

Blue Dolphin Publishing
1992

Published by Blue Dolphin Publishing, Inc.
P.O. Box 1908, Nevada City, CA 95959

ISBN: 0-931892-24-4

Library of Congress Cataloging-in-Publication Data

Figone, Liana Giovannini, 1931-
    Tastes of Tuscany : treasured family recipes and
    vignettes from the heartland of Italy / Liana
    Giovannini Figone.
        320 p.   cm.
    Includes bibliographical references and index.
    ISBN 0-931892-24-4 : $19.95
    1. Cookery, Italian—Tuscan style.   2. Tuscany (Italy)—
    Social life and customs.   I. Title.
    TX723.2.T86F54 1991
    641.5945'5—dc20   91-16950
                                                               CIP

Printed in the United States of America by
Blue Dolphin Press, Inc., Grass Valley, California

9   8   7   6   5   4   3   2   1

Robert Romano

This book is dedicated
to the memory
of a young chef,
Robert Romano,
who, with his brother Richard,
operated Romano's Restaurant
on Lombard Street in San Francisco.

Robert died on Ash Wednesday,
February 28, 1990, at the age of 33.
A friend to all my sons,
Peter, Joseph, and Frank,
a young friend who died too young.

*Liana G. Figone and her husband of
thirty-eight years, Aldo P. Figone*

About The Author

Liana Giovannini Figone was born in San Francisco,
California. She is a graduate of Presentation Grammar
School, Notre Dame Des Victoires High School, and Munson
School for Private Secretaries. She also attended City College
of San Francisco. She instituted the First Columbus Day
Beauty Pageant in San Francisco. She was president of the
Italian Catholic Federation, Branch 50, four times and served
in every office. She was president of the Women of the
Motion Picture Industry in San Francisco for eight years and
"Press Gal" for Variety Club of Northern California. Liana
received the title of Cavaliere from the Republic of Italy in
1976 and the Gold Medal from the City of Lucca for her
philanthropic work on behalf of the Italian community of
San Francisco.

Maternal	Paternal
Gemma Franceschi	Giuseppe Giorgi
Giovannini	Giovannini

LIANA G. FIGONE and ALDO FIGONE
(Peter, Joseph, Frank)

Uncles	1. Frank Franceschi	1. Silvio Giovannini
	2. Claude Franceschi	2. Arturo Giovannini
		3. Remo Giovannini
		4. Caterina Sargentini
		5. Ada Marchesini
		6. Maria Micheli
		7. Lola Giovannini
Cousins	1. Sally Franceschi	
	Roselli	1. Linda Giovannini
	1a. Peter Fransceschi	2. - 0 -
	2. Richard	3a. Christian
	Franceschi	Giovannini
	2a. Claudette Young	3b. Linda Giovannini
	2b. Rosalie Thorton	4a. Gloria Muschi
		4b. Lola Manzella
		5. Egidio Marchesini
		& 1 daughter
		6. Aldo Micheli
		7. -0-

Cousins'		
Children	1. Stephen Roselli	4a. Lorine D'Agostino
	1. Paula Kelly	4a. Lisa Muschi
	1a. Laura Franceschi	4b. Janet Bartholomew
	1a. Roy Franceschi	5. 1 son
	2. Laura Franceschi	6. -0-
	2a. Joe, Gayle, Paul Gordon & James Young	
	2b. Marc, Randolph and Troy Thorton	

The Regions of Italy

1 Piedmont
2 Aosta Valley
3 Lombardy
4 Trentino-Alto Adige
5 Venetia
6 Friull-Venetia Julia
7 Liguria
8 Emilia-Romagna
9 Tuscany
10 Umbria
11 The Marches
12 Latium
13 Abruzzo

14 Moilse
15 Campania
16 Apulla
17 Basilicata
18 Calabria
19 Sicily
20 Sardinia

Table of Contents

Bartolomeo Platina, Vatican Librarian,
published the first known cookbook in 1475.

Via Del Fosso, one of Lucca's main streets

Italian Apennines

Introduction

Tuscans are a race of very proud people who claim to have taught the Romans everything they needed to know to build the greatest empire on earth. The Tuscans also claim that every other province of Italy assimilated the accents and habits of their neighbors—the Genovese from the French, the Venetians from the Austrians, the people of the Adriatic from the Greeks—but not the Tuscans. They were there before anyone else, having settled in northern Italy in 900 B.C. They have even gone so far as to state that the Garden of Eden was located in Tuscany, that Mary, after her son's death, settled in Tuscany, and that the son of a friend of hers from Tuscany became the second pope, Linus, in 67 A.D.

The city of Lucca (where Linus was from) is one of the most beautiful cities of Tuscany and was, at one time, the capital of Italy. Its citizens still have a special kind of pride. The city is surrounded by walls topped by a shaded avenue and whether they come from "inside the walls or outside the walls" they still say they are "Lucchesi."

The Tuscans had many sons with a claim to fame, among them Amerigo Vespucci, for whom America was named, and Giovanni da Verrazano, for whom New York's famous bridge was named. Both were Florentines. Other famous Tuscans include: Filippo Mazzei, a friend of Thomas Jefferson, who helped write the U.S. Constitution; Giacomo Puccini, who was born in Lucca and lived most of his life at Torre Del Lago (Viareggio), where he wrote his first opera, *Manon Lescaut;* Piero della Francesca (modern name Peter Franceschi), world-famous artist; and Salvatore Ferragamo, who set up his shoemaking shop on Via Tornabuoni in Florence.

Tuscan cooking is the forerunner of France's *haute cusine.* When Caterina dei Medici (wife of Henry II) left Livorno (Leghorn) for Marseilles in 1533 and became queen of France, she brought thirty-five cooks with her, and they in turn taught the French the art of gastronomy. From that point on, the food of the royal house of France lost its plainness and became more of a noble cuisine.

Judge for yourself, for no cookbook author can really lay claim to the invention of a recipe, but rather only to being the collector of these recipes. The recipes in this book are an accumulation from family and friends.

As far as Tuscans are concerned, the Lord's promise of plenty in *Deuteronomy* could very well have been written for us: "He will give the rain for your land in its season . . . that you may gather in your grain, your wine and your oil. And he will give grass in your fields for your cattle."

In retrospect, for the purpose at hand, that of compiling a cookbook, I had three lucky breaks. First, I was a Depression baby of an Italian family. This meant that even though funds may have been low, Italian families wanted their children to eat well. The Tuscan staples of beans, polenta, and rice, simply combined, came to good stead.

Second, my father at one time or another either owned his own restaurant or worked for some famous restaurants of the time. His restaurant, The Universe, was located on Broadway Street in San Francisco between Kearny and Montgomery Streets. He subsequently worked for The Backyard, which was owned by Bob Scalabrino; Larry's, which was owned by Larry Salarpi; and Alfred's, 886 Broadway, which had a variety of owners. My father held various positions in these establishments. I remember one of his favorite sayings, "Everybody's a chef, but nobody knows how to cook." Those were the days when aspiring cooks were trained under the master chefs and were not products of culinary academies.

Third, after I was married, being an only daughter and only child, I was expected to have the "family" every Sunday for lunch or dinner. Usually, there was my husband Aldo, myself, our sons Peter and Joseph (and later our son Frank), my mother and father, my grandmother, my paternal uncle Silvio Giovannini, who worked at the Fior D'Italia Restaurant, and my maternal uncle Claude Franceschi, who worked at the Shadows and later owned his own restaurant, The Barbary, on Pacific Street. With every subsequent year, my weight would increase, the conclusion being that anyone who is overweight loves to eat and loves to cook. Over the years, I was asked for recipes and finally decided to put them all together for the benefit of those who asked for them, and for the enjoyment of you who have purchased this book.

Today's genealogists often refer to "family genes." Ironically, my mother's family were "Franceschis"

(Della Francesca). A Dr. Franceschi cultivated the barren soil of the area today known as Santa Barbara, California. He introduced foreign and exotic plants to the area and was successful in growing them in that arid territory. There is a street named Franceschi in Santa Barbara. Our son Joseph, a grandson of the Franceschi's, was Manager of Cost Plus Nurseries at Fisherman's Wharf in San Francisco.

On my father's side of the family (Giovannini), through many years of genealogical research, we lay claim to Medici family roots with modern day connections to the city of Siena and to the Dukes of Emmery in Lyons, France.

This book has been compiled with the patience of my husband Aldo, my sons Peter Joseph, Joseph Enrico, and Frank Joseph, and with the help of many relatives both living and deceased—my father Joseph Giovannini, my mother Gemma Franceschi Giovannini, my grandmother and grandfather Enrichetta and Egildo Franceschi, my maternal uncles Frank and Claude Franceschi, my paternal uncle Silvio Giovannini, the cousins, who had patience and waited while I was "busy" writing the book, Richard Franceschi, his wife, Sherri, Linda Giovannini, and the closest of friends, Gloria Parenti Romano and Maria Barsotti Della Santina.

An Italian-American mother spends her life as follows: 90% of it waiting for her sons to find "the right girl" and 10% of it waiting for the first grandchild. "Is something wrong with you?"

So far, I haven't had much luck: Peter is 34—single; Joseph is 29—single; Frank is 25—single.

All these recipes couldn't go to waste. The "right girl" must be out there someplace. If there is a second cookbook, hopefully it'll be dedicated to the "right girl." I'll even settle for a non-Italian with a non-Italian name, something like "Kimberly."

When I was in college our journalism teacher would say, "Always write about what you know."

So what happened? When my recipes had been collected from family members and friends, the bookshelfs got crowded, the scrapbooks were bulging, and there was no way to go except a computer. I enjoyed the many hours of programming, and I hope you enjoy the time you spend reviewing, preparing, and presenting the food to your family and friends.

My love of cooking started with "Nonna Bella" Enrichetta Franceschi, who spent many years as a housewife in the San Joaquin Valley of California preparing food for ranch hands and for guests who would drop in from the "City," the city being San Francisco. Even though it took close to five hours to cross the bay by ferryboat and then drive through Oakland, Hayward, Dublin, Livermore, etc., there wasn't a weekend when someone from the City didn't manage to find their way to the valley. During the week, Nonna would spend hours preparing lunch for the men who worked on the ranch cutting asparagus, boxing it, and shipping it either to the plants where they would be processed by the U.S. Army for the soldiers who were fighting the Second World War or to the produce markets in San Francisco.

THE LILY OF·THE VALLEY — ASPARAGUS

When the first Tuscan immigrants settled in the San Joaquin Valley, they carried with them from Tuscany, moist, dirt-filled pouches containing crowns of their treasured lilies, asparagus.

The crowns were and are planted under four inches of dirt and after ten months they produce ferns. When the frost of winter appears, the ferns die and the stalks remain. The cutting period increases each year and by the fourth year the cutting period lasts about ninety days.

Asparagus, which have been cultivated in Italy since the days of the Roman Empire, will not produce if exposed to pesticides. They are a member of the lily family along with onions, leeks and garlic.

The green variety of our lily is a California favorite and owes its deep green color to the combination of winter frost and sunshine. In Italy the white variety is highly prized. The white stalks result from no exposure to the sun. The plants are covered with straw and loose soil.

A favorite way to cook the asparagus is to wrap the trimmed and cleaned spears in aluminum foil with pats of butter, securing the ends of the foil and baking the packages in a 350 degree oven for 40 minutes. This is especially time-saving if you are in the process of baking a chicken or beef roast.

I think it would be appropriate to start this cookbook with an asparagus recipe.

Asparagus Frittata

1 quart	water
1 teaspoon	salt
12	asparagus, cleaned
½ cup	olive oil
1 link	Italian sausage, removed from casing and crumbled
1 clove	garlic, minced
½ cup	red onion, minced
to taste	salt and pepper
4	eggs, slightly beaten

To 1 quart water add 1 teaspoon salt. Bring to a boil. Add asparagus. Boil 5 minutes, drain and set aside.

Put the olive oil in heavy skillet, heat on low heat. Add Italian sausage. When sausage is no longer pink, add garlic and red onion. Add asparagus cut in ½ inch sections. Stir well. Sprinkle with salt and pepper to taste. Simmer for 2 minutes. Pour the eggs over mixture. Cover with lid. Cook over low heat twenty minutes. Remove from heat, let cool. The eggs will set while cooling.

*The author
with
first cousins
Richard
Franceschi
and
Linda
Giovannini*

While the eastern part of the United States was populated mainly by immigrants from other regions, the Tuscans immigrated to California either to work in the fertile San Joaquin Valley as tillers of the land or as cooks in the San Francisco Bay Area, the Mother Lode's gold fields, or in the camps set up for the workers who were instrumental in connecting the eastern and western United States by railroad tracks. My fathers' grandfather, Giuseppe Giovannini, came to San Francisco and here married a Genovese girl, Caterina Cavagliato, and then returned to Italy and purchased sixteen miles of lumber country at Pievepelago in the Italian Apennines.

The San Francisco Bay Area today hosts our favorite following restaurants that feature, either wholly or in part, northern Italian Food. Even though all the owners may not be Tuscan, they have on their menus some of that beautiful Tuscan connection.

BUCA GIOVANNI, Greenwich St., S.F.
CAESARS, Bay at Powell, S.F.
DEER PARK, Fairfax, Calif.
DI GRANDE'S, Taraval St., S.F.
ETRUSCA, Spear St., S.F.
FIRENZE, Stockton St., S.F.
GOLD MIRROR, Taraval St., S.F.
GRIFONE, Powell St., S.F.
MANZELLA'S LOFT, Hayward, Calif.
MARIN JOE'S, Corte Madera, Calif.
MAYES OYSTER HOUSE, Polk St., S.F.
MILANO, Pacific St., S.F.
NEW PISA, Green St., S.F.
NEW SAN REMO, Mason St., S.F.
NORTH BEACH RESTAURANT, Stockton St., S.F.
OSTERIA TOSCANA, Sacramento St., S.F.

PANE É VINO, Steiner St., S.F.
STOCKTON JOE'S, Stockton, Calif.
THE WATERFRONT, Pier 7, S.F.
WESTLAKE JOE'S, Daly City, Calif.

Now, plan ahead. . . . You're going to have a big dinner in about a month. Maybe it's the first time the in-laws are coming to your house, or maybe you're having your friends from work. Whatever the reason, you should start planning about a month ahead. If you have just set up housekeeping and you "love to cook," you can probably look forward to a lifetime of entertaining. So start out right. Buy yourself a package of 3 x 5-inch cards (it's easier to save your recipes on cards). File them by categories. Mine were filed as follows:

Antipasti and Insalata (appetizers and salads)
Pesce (fish)
Primi (usually soup, pasta, or rice)
Secondi (main course)
Dolci (desserts)
Varie (miscellaneous)

A TAVOLA NON SI INVECCHIA MAI
We never age at the dinner table

*Preparing
for Festa
Di Santa
Croce*

Walls of Lucca

THE REGIONS OF TUSCANY
AND THE SPECIALTIES EACH IS NOTED FOR

FIRENZE: Bistecca alla Fiorentina, zuppa di magro, trippa alla fiorentina, fagioli all'olio, piselli al prosciutto, finocchiona, zuppa di fagioli, strisce di ceci, ranocchi fritti, braciole di maiale, castrato bollito, zampa di vitello alla fiorentina, animelle di vitello coi funghi, cappelle di funghi alla griglia, minestrone toscano, asparagi all'olio, fave stufate, fagioli e caviale, lombatina di vitella, stracotto alla fiorentina, castagnaccio, fritelle di farina dolce, stiacciata unta.

AREZZO: Capretto arrosto, fegatelli alla toscana, pappardelle all'aretina, arista all'aretina, galantina di pollo in gelatina, trote del Casentino alla casalinga, pecorino della Val Tiberina, bistecche al carbone, agnellotti, cacciagione, cappone in galantina, pollo alla cacciatora, fagioli all'uccelletto.

SIENA: arrostino misto alla senese, fritto di pollo e carciofi, fritto di cervello e carciofi, polli allo spiedo, trippa alla senese, salsicce e salami, pecorino, bistecca alla cacciatora, cannoli, tortelli, bocconcini, pollo fritto, tortino di carciofi, panforte, Ricciarelli, Cavallucci, copate, fiori di Siena, Torta di Cecco.

SAN GIMIGNANO: Pollo e vitello alla marsala, polli allo spiedo, risotto con sugo di carne, agnello al forno.

MONTECARLO: crostini, risotto, cacciagione al girarrosto, girati di pollo, arista di maiale, capretto e faraona, prosciutto di montagna, agnellotti, pecorino della Val di Nievole, castagnaccio.

LUCCA: crostini, zuppa di magro, pollo al mattone, petti di pollo, tortelli alla toscana, capretto alla casalinga, tortelli di magro, fricassea di pollo, pollo alla griglia, arrosto morto di manzo, fagioli al fiasco, minestrone toscano, testa di vitella, lingua, spezzati alla casalinga, buccellato, pan di ramerino, zuccotto, castagnaccio con ricotta fresca.

MARINA DI PISA: risotto nero, risotto ai frutti di mare, arselle, cieche alla pisana, pesce di Bocca d'Arno.

PISA: zuppa di magro alla pisana, stoccafisso al pomodoro alla pisana, fegatini e piselli, fritto alla pisana, zuppa di fagioli, fegatini di pollo alla salvia, cieche alla pisana, petti di pollo al funghetto, pollo al mattone, pesce fritto, zuccotto.

PISTOIA: pappardelle al sugo di lepre, crostini, faraona al cartoccio, arista sott'olio, bistecca, pollo alla griglia, faraona alla griglia, capriolo, cacciagione, tagliatelle, castagnaccio, frittelle di farina di castagne.

LIVORNO: triglie alla livornese, cacciucco alla livornese, triglie al cartoccio, allo spiedo, fritte; spiedini di scampi e totani, baccalá alla livornese, baccalá al pomodoro, antipasti di mare, aragoste, risotto alla marinara, orate al forno, spaghetti con le vongole, frutti di mare, sogliole, dentice, spigole, cernie alla griglia, zuppa di arselle.

VIAREGGIO: cacciucco alla viareggina, risotto di pesce, spaghetti con le vongole, gamberetti alla marinara, totani con le cipolle, muscoli alla marinara, spiedini di scampi, fritto di totani e scampi, antipasti di mare, fritto misto, insalata di frutti di mare, scampi allo spiedo, zuppa di datteri, spiedini di gamberoni, insalata di cernie, funghi dell'alta Versilia arrosto, spezzatino di maiale, castagnaccio, zuccotto.

TORRE DEL LAGO PUCCINI: crostini di milza, crostini di caccia, folaghe alla Puccini, cacciucco di pollo, germano arrosto, anitra arrosto, pappardelle alla lepre, cacciagione, pollo alla griglia.

SAN VICENZO: insalate di pesce, arrosti di cinghiale, insalate, pollo, girarrosti, pollo alla griglia.

GROSSETO: cinghiale in dolce e forte, girarrosti, cacciagione, prosciutto e salame di cinghiale, capocollo di cinghiale, salsicce di cinghiale, spaghetti alla buttera, faraona, lepre in dolce e forte, capretto, polli all spiedo, pappardelle alla lepre, faraona, fagianata, bistecce, pappardelle al cinghiale, tortelli di ricotta, triglie alla marinara.

CHI PRIMA ARRIVA, PRIMA ALLOGGIA
Who first arrives, will be the first welcomed.

Walls of Lucca

A typical street in Lucca

My mother and father's generation came to America from Lucca, Italy. Lucca lies between Siena and Florence, and even though it is a small town within walls which at one time were surrounded by moats and entered through gates, everyone who comes from the surrounding towns claims that they are from Lucca. My mother's family of her immediate generation was from Pieve San Paolo and my father's from Ponte Della Madalena, aka Ponte Del Diavolo, Borgo A Mozzano. Here in San Francisco we have our own club which is called L'Associazione Lucchesi Nel Mondo and which boasts some of our area's most famous Tuscan residents such as Romano Della Santina, who was first president of the club and is the owner of Marin Joe's, a restaurant across the Golden Gate Bridge in Corte Madera. Other club members have included Frank Petrini, owner of Petrini's Markets; Lou Martinelli of Florence Delicatessen and Florence Fine Foods; Franco Santucci of Stella Pastry; Romano Buoncristiani of Victoria Pasty; Domenico Tintori of Food for Less, Tracy, Calif.; Sergio Pardini of Pardini's Market, San Rafael, Calif.; and numerous others. The club is open to anyone who originates from Lucca and is an international club with branches in Australia, Argentina, England, throughout Europe, South America, and the United States.

Lucca lies in the center of Tuscany. Tuscany is one of Italy's large areas consisting of nine provinces (Arezzo, Firenze, Grosetto, Livorno, Lucca, Massa Carrara, Pisa, Pistoia, and Siena), and the Island of Elba. The food of Tuscany is very uncomplicated. In America when a recipe says it is "alla Fiorentina" it usually means that spinach is used. However, in Florence it means in the Florentine style and doesn't necessarily have spinach in it. Because of very few large ranches, the Tuscan cooking most frequently used small animals and vegetables. Chianti is the wine that is best known from the Tuscan region and the Chianti region lies in the area around Siena.

I have purposely omitted any mention of wines as I feel unqualified in that area. However, wines from the Chianti region in Tuscany and our own California wines, added to most recipes, will only enhance your dish. So experiment with white wines for fish and poultry and red wine with meats by adding a small amount, usually 8 ounces, while recipe is at the simmering stage.

The most essential items in the kitchen, I feel, are a good cleaver, a good chopping board, and a small herb garden. You will note that food processors and microwaves are seldom used.

Throughout the book, I have purposely omitted the amount each recipe serves. What serves four Italian men will probably serve six "Americani."

È MEGLIO RICEVERLE CHE FARLE
It's better to receive them than cause them

Photo by Rusty and Dolores Enos

Pictured above, standing left to right: Romano Della Santina, owner of Marin Joe's at Corte Madera, California (Romano originates from Pieve San Paolo, Lucca, Italy); Aldo Figone (the author's husband); the author. Seated left to right: The author's mother, Gemma Giovannini (who also originates from Pieve San Paolo and is distantly related to Romano and his wife) and Maria Barsotti Della Santina, Romano's wife, who originates from Santa Margherita (Lucca) Italy.

Antipasti
e Insalate

(Appetizers and Salads)

A housewife shopping in an outdoor market

OGNI CAMPANILE SUONA LE SUE CAMPANE
Every bell tower rings its own bell

Antipasto
(Pickled Vegetables in
Tomato Sauce with Tuna)

One of my favorite recipes is one for ANTIPASTO. This is a mixture, made approximately one month before you plan to use it. The recipe comes from the cookbook Herbs for the Kitchen, *which was written by a dear friend of my mother and father, Irma Goodrich Mazza. Irma and her husband Mario were two of my parents' best friends and were often guests as I was growing up. Mario sang a beautiful rendition of the Lord's Prayer at my wedding. They were both present at many family celebrations, including my mother's eightieth birthday party at Caesar's Restaurant here in San Francisco.*

This recipe was one of my first successful tries at cooking, one of the first I used after my marriage thirty-eight years ago. I have taken the liberty of making just a change or two due to the availability of the staples in our area.

Those flat round cans of antipasto imported from Italy are good eating but costly for regular consumption. To can a supply for your family is not too much of a trick if this recipe is used. The vinegar and spices preclude spoilage, so it is not necessary to can under pressure.

1 pound each	celery in 1 inch pieces
	cauliflower cut by stems
	sliced carrots
1-15 ounce can	wax beans
1-9 ounce jar	pearl onions
1-6 ounce jar	artichoke hearts
1-15 ounce can	pitted black olives
2 quarts	cider vinegar
6-8 ounce cans	tomato sauce
3 cups	tomato juice
2 cups	olive oil
1 tablespoon	whole black pepper
3-8 ounce cans	button mushrooms
1-4 ounce jar	capers, drained
1-12 ounce jar	small sour gherkins
4-2 ounce cans	anchovie fillets
1-12 ounce jar	little pickled peppers
	(peperoncini)
4-6½ ounce cans	solid tuna packed in vegetable
	or olive oil
	enough water to produce liquid
	to cover entire mixture

The night before canning, cook all raw vegetables in equal amounts of water and vinegar for 10 minutes. Drain well overnight. The next morning combine tomato sauce, tomato juice, olive oil, and black pepper. Cook together 10 minutes, stirring well. Add everything else but the tuna and the anchovies. Boil 10 minutes, then pack ingredients into hot, sterilized jar (run jars through dishwasher and remove one at a time). Try to distribute ingredients evenly in jars. Push two generous chunks of tuna and fillets down under the sauce in each jar just before sealing. To seal, keep lids in a pan at a rolling boil. Remove one lid at a time, put on jar, and seal with ring. The longer the antipasto stands, at least one month, the better. However, there have been occasions when I have had to use it within a few days, and our guests still said it was great.

Antipasto di Finocchio (Fennel Appetizer)

1 bulb	fennel
4 tablespoons	olive oil
1 tablespoon	lemon juice
to taste	salt and
	freshly ground black pepper

Soak head of fennel in very cold water with a few ice cubes for 2 or 3 hours. Slice very thin and pile slices in a dish. Cover with olive oil, lemon juice, salt, and pepper.

Avocados Riempiti con Noce (Avocados Stuffed with Walnuts)

6 ounces	shelled walnuts, halves
4	ripe avocados
1 tablespoon	lemon juice
4 tablespoons	whipped cream
to taste	salt and pepper

Finely chop walnuts reserving 8 halves. Cut avocado in half, removing pit. Remove pulp without cutting shell. Mash pulp with chopped walnuts and combine with lemon juice, whipped cream, salt, and pepper. Return pulp to avocado shells and top each with one walnut half. Cover with plastic wrap and keep in refrigerator at least 2 hours. Serve as a salad.

Condimento per Insalate (Dressing for Salads)

1 tablespoon	each salt and pepper
1 cup	red wine vinegar
4 cups	olive oil
1 tablespoon	mayonnaise
1 tablespoon	tomato sauce or catsup

Put salt and pepper in a bowl and pour in red wine vinegar. Stir until salt dissolves. Add about four times as much olive oil as vinegar. Add mayonnaise and tomato sauce or catsup. Stir lightly to blend (do not beat).

CANTA CHE TI PASSA
Sing and it will pass

Crostini con Fegati di Pollo (Bread Rounds with Chicken Livers)

14 slices	French bread
1 cube	butter, reserve 2 tablespoons
1 pound	chicken livers, chopped
3 tablespoons	olive oil
5	fresh sage leaves, finely chopped
3	anchovy fillets
6	capers

Toast bread; spread with butter on both sides. Clean and wash chicken livers and dry with paper towels. Put olive oil in pan with 2 tablespoons of butter. Add sage leaves and liver. Cook five minutes. Remove pan from heat and let mixture cool. Chop liver, sage, juices, anchovies, and capers. Grind until smooth and spread on bread. Place under boiler until brown.

Crostini di Formaggio (Bread Rounds with Cheese)

1	baguette bread, thinly sliced
2 bunches	green onions, thinly sliced to just below green stem, reserving green stems
1 cup	mayonnaise
1 cup	Parmesan cheese, grated
½ cup	sour cream
1 teaspoon	Worcestershire sauce
to taste	salt and pepper
sprinkle	paprika

Buy a baguette bread in any bakery. These are the long thin breads. Cut at an angle into thin slices. Slice white part of onions lengthwise and then chop. Put in bowl, add mayonnaise, Parmesan cheese, sour cream, Worcestershire sauce, salt, and pepper. Mix well. Spread this mixture on thin slices of bread and put under broiler until they turn brown. Remove from broiler with spatula and sprinkle with paprika. Place on platter. Garnish with thinly sliced green onion stems.

Cura di Olive (Curing Green Olives)

for 12 pounds

15 pounds (approximately)	green olives
1-12 ounce can	lye
2½ cups	salt
1½ cups	additional salt

In a 5-gallon terracotta crock pot, put green olives to the halfway mark. Fill pot with cold water. For 5 gallons put in 1 can of lye. Make sure solution completely covers olives even though a few will pop up to the surface. Stir several times a day. In about 12 hours, start cutting into an olive to check lye penetration. When lye has penetrated to the pit (you'll see a slight yellow tinge), drain off solution. NOTE: Use rubber gloves when working with lye solutions.

Now you have a crock pot with just olives in it. Fill pot with cold water again. Add 2½ cups of salt (no lye this time). Keep olives in this solution for 72 hours, stirring frequently. Again, make sure solution covers olives. Drain off solution again. Fill pot with cold water again. Add 1½ cups salt. Keep olives in this solution at least 4 days. Keep olives covered (add water if some water evaporates) and stir frequently, about 6 times a day. Olives can now be eaten.

CANNING: You can leave the olives in the crock pot with plain water after draining off the last solution and replacing with cold water, but if you want to keep them indefinitely, it is better to jar them. To jar, make a solution of 1 cup salt to 1 gallon water and bring to a boil. Put about 1 quart of olives in a sieve and put this in boiling water for 1 minute. Meanwhile, in another pot on the stove, make a solution of ¼ cup salt to 1 gallon of water and just heat to boiling point.* Run jars through dishwasher and remove one at a time while still hot. Put olives in a jar to ½ inch from top. Add solution (the last, ½ cup salt to 2 gallons of water or the pickling one if you prefer) to just cover olives. Put on a lid that has been dipped in boiling water for 2 minutes and screw on cap. If you buy caning jars, buy 1-quart size, complete with lids and screw-on caps. This recipe makes about 12 jars, depending on size of olives.

*PICKLING: If you prefer a stronger solution, at this point take:

2-1.25 ounce cans	pickling spice
1 rind of	lemon (cut in strips)
1 stick	cinnamon
1	bay leaf
4	cloves
6	peppercorns

Tie above ingredients in a cloth, add to water. Boil water 20 minutes, squeezing cloth two or three times so flavors penetrates water.

Olives ready to be cured

CHI VA PER INGANNARE
RIMANE INGANNATO
Who deceives, is deceived

Foglie di Finocchio (Fennel Leaves)

1	fennel bulb
4 ounces	ricotta cheese
6 whole	anchovies (under salt), bought in Italian delicatessen split, and cleaned of salt coating, finely chopped
½ cup	vinegar
½ cup	olive oil
to taste	salt and pepper

Break apart fennel leaves. Spread with ricotta cheese and top with anchovies. Make a mixture of equal parts of vinegar and olive oil, salt and pepper. Pour mixture over leaves.

Funghi Ripieni
(Stuffed Mushroom Caps)

Take **one pound of mushroom caps** (break off and reserve stems). Saute caps in some **melted butter**. Drain and cool.

Combine:

1-6½ ounce can	**minced clams**
1-8 ounce package	**cream cheese**
¼ pound	**prosciutto slice, chopped**
½ cup	**Parmesan cheese, grated**
to taste	**salt and pepper**
reserved	**mushroom stems, chopped**
¼ teaspoon	**Worcestershire sauce**
¼ cup	**fresh marjoram**

Stuff mushroom caps and place under broiler until lightly browned. Any leftover stuffing can be spread on slices of bread and broiled.

ALTERNATE STUFFING:

6	**green onions, chopped**
1 clove	**garlic, chopped fine**
¼ slice	**prosciutto, chopped**
1 tablespoon	**parsley, chopped**
to taste	**salt and pepper**
1 teaspoon	**dried marjoram**

¼ cup   white wine
½ cup   bread crumbs

Saute green onions and garlic in olive oil until tender. Combine with prosciutto, parsley, salt, pepper, marjoram, white wine, and bread crumbs until mixture is just spreadable.

Mushrooms on display

Insalata alla Cesare (Caesar Salad)

1 large head	Romaine lettuce, torn in pieces
2 cloves	garlic
2	eggs
¼ teaspoon	dry mustard
¼ cup	olive oil
½	lemon, juiced
1 tablespoon	wine vinegar
6	anchovies (under salt), bought in Italian delicatessen split, and cleaned of salt coating
¼ cup	Parmesan cheese, grated
to taste	black pepper, coarsely ground
to taste	salt
½ cup	croutons

Dry lettuce thoroughly. Cut garlic cloves in half and rub them all over the inside of a large wooden salad bowl; discard garlic. Cook eggs gently in simmering water for 1 minute from simmering point. When cool enough to handle, break eggs into salad bowl and mix rapidly with a spoon until well blended and light in color. Add dry mustard and stir, then slowly pour oil into egg mixture. Add lemon juice and vinegar; mix well. Toss lettuce and add mixture. Toss again. Cut anchovies in pieces and add to salad. Toss again. Sprinkle salad with cheese, salt, and pepper. Add croutons.

Insalata di Acciughe (Anchovie Salad)

4 small	Roma tomatoes
4	cauliflower flowers
1	lemon, juiced (reserve half)
8 slices	French bread
1 clove	garlic, cut in half
about a dozen	pitted black olives
3	anchovies (under salt) bought in Italian delicatessen, split, remove salt coating and wash under running water
6 or 7 leaves	Romaine lettuce
4 tablespoons	olive oil
1 tablespoon	vinegar
to taste	salt and pepper

Wash, peel, and cut tomatoes in quarters. Wash cauliflower flowers and slice thin. Sprinkle lemon juice over cauliflower. Toast French bread and rub each slice with garlic clove. Drain olives. Wash and drain salad and cut in strips. Mix salad with tomatoes, cauliflower, olives, and anchovies. In a small bowl mix oil, vinegar, salt, pepper, and reserved lemon juice. Pour over salad. Serve with toasted bread.

Insalata di Pane
(Bread Salad)

1 large	red onion
10 large	fresh basil leaves
2 large	ripe tomatoes
1 loaf	stale bread
to taste	salt and pepper
½ cup	olive oil
½ cup	vinegar

Peel skin from onion and wash carefully. Wash basil leaves and tomatoes. Soak bread in cold water with tomatoes, onion, and basil for 20 minutes, then squeeze bread to remove liquid. Cut onion in quarters and finely slice each quarter. Place onion pieces on soaked and drained bread. Tear each basil leaf into two or three pieces and arrange over onions. Dice tomatoes into squares and place on top of basil. Put everything in a covered container and place in refrigerator until thoroughly chilled. Remove from refrigerator and transfer contents to bowl. Season with salt, pepper, oil, and vinegar. Mix thoroughly.

Insalata di Spinaci Crudi (Spinach Salad)

3 bunches	fresh spinach, torn in bite size pieces
6 thin slices	prosciutto, fried crisp, drained and crumbled (reserve drippings)
¼ cup	green onions, chopped
⅓ cup	vinegar
⅓ cup	water
1 package	Italian dressing mix
2 teaspoons	sugar
2	hard boiled eggs, chopped

Place spinach in salad bowl. Add prosciutto and onions and toss. To prosciutto drippings add vinegar, water, Italian dressing mix and sugar. Heat to boiling, then cool. Pour over spinach mixture and toss thoroughly. Add eggs and toss again. Serve immediately.

Insalata Estiva (Summer Salad)

½ cup	vinegar
¾ cup	olive oil
to taste	salt and pepper
1 teaspoon	sugar
2 dozen stalks	asparagus, cooked al dente (i.e. crisp)
1 pound	string beans, cooked and drained
6	artichoke hearts (from can or jar)
3	ripe tomatoes, peeled and quartered
1 small	cucumber, peeled and thinly sliced
10 leaves	fresh basil, cut in thin strips

Mix vinegar and olive oil with salt, pepper and sugar. Place the next five ingredients in salad bowl; pour on oil and vinegar dressing. Toss lightly, top with basil strips, and serve.

Melanzane in Salamoia (Pickled Eggplant)

1	eggplant, peeled and cut into shoestring pieces
to taste	salt
2 cups	white vinegar
3 cups	olive oil
1 clove	garlic, minced
½ teaspoon	red pepper flakes, crushed
1 tablespoon	fresh oregano leaves, chopped

Put the eggplant in colander, sprinkle with salt. Leave overnight with weight on top to remove all liquid.

Boil vinegar, add eggplant and let cool for 24 hours. Drain off vinegar, put in dish and marinate with oil, minced garlic, pinch of crushed red pepper and oregano. Place in small jars and add olive oil to cover and seal, will keep indefinitely.

TUSCANY is bordered on the northwest by La Spezia (Genova) and on the northeast by Emilia Romagna.

When I first met my husband and my father found out that Aldo's family was from La Spezia, he wasn't really thrilled about having a son-in-law who was not from Tuscany. You have to understand that when Garibaldi united Italy in the 1800s, he united it into one nation, but there are still and probably always will be prejudice between one region and another.

Well, as it happened, Monsignor Giorgi, my father's cousin who appears elsewhere in this book, had access to all the family records and, when my sons were born, I become more interested in family roots. My great grandfather had come to the United States in the early 1800s and had married a girl from La Spezia here in San Francisco by the name of Caterina Cavagliato and then returned to Italy. Another great grandfather had married a girl from La Spezia named Maria Galetti, making my father part Genovese on two sides. From that time on, he never distinguished my husband as being "Genovese."

E MEGLIO ESSERE INVIDIATI CHE COMPATITI
It is better to be envied than to be pitied

Melone e Prosciutto (Melon and Italian Ham)

Instead of a salad, we sometimes serve melon and prosciutto before a meal. The way we do this is by buying thin slices of prosciutto and wrapping the prosciutto around thin wedges of melon with skin removed. Prosciutto is also served wrapped around fresh figs.

Joseph E. Figone holding up the Leaning Tower of Pisa

Ostriche con Prosciutto e Cipolline (Oysters with Italian Ham and Chives)

3 dozen	oysters in shells
¼ pound	prosciutto slice, cut in small cubes
2 tablespoons	Champagne or white wine
½ cup	butter, melted
½ cup	red wine
3 tablespoons	chives, chopped

Bake oysters at 350 degrees until slightly opened. Remove top part of shell and place small piece of prosciutto on each oyster. Lower oven to 200 degrees and bake oysters several minutes longer or until prosciutto is warm. Pour champagne or white wine into saucepan and bring to boil. Cool. Whisk butter into wine, returning to low heat if necessary to keep butter smooth. Add chives and spoon mixture over each oyster. Serve warm.

Pandorato alla Crema di Formaggio (Fried Bread with Cheese Sauce)

4 ounces	Monterey Jack cheese, cut in small pieces
2	egg yolks, beaten
1 tablespoon	butter
2	egg whites, beaten
6 slices	bread
1 cup	flour
½ cup	olive oil

Put Monterey Jack cheese in the top of a double boiler. Add egg yolks and stir with a wooden spoon until well mixed, creamy, and warm. Remove from fire and stir in butter. To fry bread, trim crusts, dip in water then in flour then in egg whites. Fry in hot olive oil on both sides until golden brown. Lay in a flat dish and spread with cheese mixture.

Pane Fritto con Acciughe (Fried Bread with Anchovies)

For each person:

2 slices	white bread
1 tablespoon	blue cheese, softened
2	anchovies, cut into bits
2	eggs
to taste	salt and pepper
½ cup	olive oil
½ cup	milk
½ cup	flour

For each person take two slices of white bread; trim crusts. Spread one slice with blue cheese and bits of anchovies. Top with other slice and cut in half. In a deep bowl beat the eggs, salt and pepper to taste. Heat olive oil in a pan. Dip sandwich in milk, beaten eggs, and then in flour. Fry quickly, first on one side and then the other until golden brown. Serve very hot.

Sixth century
Cathedral of
Lucca San Martino

The walls surrounding Lucca

Pizza alla Toscana
(Tuscan Version of Pizza)

1 package	dry yeast
½ teaspoon	sugar
1 cup	warm water
2 tablespoons	vegetable oil
1 teaspoon	salt
1 teaspoon	dried red pepper flakes
¼ cup	parsley, chopped
2½ cups	flour
½ cup	cornmeal
3 cloves	garlic, minced
2 tablespoons	olive oil

Dissolve yeast and sugar in ½ cup warm water. Add remaining water, oil, salt, red pepper flakes, parsley, flour and cornmeal. Beat vigorously. Knead into ball and let rest about 10 minutes. Pat or roll into approximately 14 x 18 inch rectangle or 16 inch round pizza pan. Brush with olive oil and sprinkle with garlic.

Top with:

3 medium	tomatoes, diced
1 cup	pitted black olives, sliced
2 teaspoons	dried oregano, crumbled
to taste	salt and pepper

1 cup   mozzarella cheese, shredded
1 cup   Monterey Jack cheese, shredded
3 ounces green peperoncini, drained and
            chopped

Bake at 425 degrees 20 minutes or until dough is crispy.

Pizzette (Small Pizzas)

½ cup   olive oil
1½ cups   sharp cheese of your choice,
                 shredded
3 ounce can   black olives, sliced
3 ounce can   green peperoncini, chopped
8 ounce can   tomato sauce
⅛ teaspoon   garlic powder
¼ teaspoon   dried oregano
3   French bread rolls
3   green onions, thinly sliced

In bowl mix olive oil, sharp cheese, black olives, green peppers, tomato sauce, garlic powder and oregano. Slice hard French bread rolls to desired thickness. Spread mixture on roll slices, top with green onions. Place on cookie sheet. Place under broiler for 4 to 5 minutes or until bubbly.

Polpettine con Sugo (Meatballs with Sauce)

1 pound	ground beef
1	egg
to taste	salt
1 cup packed	brown sugar
1-8 ounce can	tomato sauce
3 tablespoons	lemon juice

Mix ground beef, beaten egg, salt, and ½ cup brown sugar in mixing bowl. Make into 1½- to 2-inch round meatballs. Place in a two- or three-quart glass baking dish. Cover with wax paper and set in microwave oven at MEDIUM HIGH power for eight minutes. Drain off extra grease. Mix tomato sauce, lemon juice, ½ cup brown sugar, and salt. Pour evenly over meatballs. Cover again with wax paper and place in microwave, same power, for additional 5 to 6 minutes. Makes 17 to 20 meatballs. Good over rice or pasta and delicious served as hors d'oeuvres.

My mother, Gemma Franceschi Giovannini, has a ranch at Tracy, California.

When recipes call for tomatoes during tomato season, we use fresh peeled tomatoes as often as possible.

When we don't have them on our ranch, we get them from other Tuscans in the area: the Dell'Ossos, the Pellegris, the Bianchis, the Giovacchinis, the Colis or the Benetti-Rochas.

It's a modern day way of bartering—fresh French bread from Rich Pinocci, Proprietor of Italian French Bakery in San Francisco, for fresh tomatoes. That's "Famiglia."

The author's mother, Gemma Franceschi Giovannini, with "Boccia."

Pomodori Tostati con Aglio e Erbette (Toasted Tomatoes with Garlic and Herbs)

8 large	firm, ripe tomatoes
12 cloves	garlic, split lengthwise into 4 pieces
½ cup	fresh bread crumbs, chopped fine
½ cup	Parmesan cheese, grated
¼ cup	fresh rosemary, thyme and oregano, combined
to taste	pepper
⅓ cup	olive oil

Slice a wafer thin cut from bottom of each tomato. Cut off about ½ inch from the top of each tomato. Stab 6 slivers of garlic into top of each tomato. Put tomatoes in a lightly greased baking pan. Mix bread crumbs, Parmesan cheese and herbs and top each tomato with mixture. Drizzle the crumb topping with a few drops of oil allowing some to drip lightly down the side of each tomato. Roast uncovered in a pre-heated 350 degree oven for 30 to 45 minutes. Tomatoes are done when tops are brown and sides lightly wrinkled.

Torta di Zucchini e Riso (Rice Zucchini Torte)

1 cup	uncooked rice
2 pounds	zucchini, sliced
½ cup	green onions, chopped
⅓ cup	parsley, chopped
½ cup	olive oil
3	eggs, well beaten
½ teaspoon	Accent
1 tablespoon	fresh rosemary, removed from stalks and chopped
1 teaspoon	garlic powder
to taste	salt and pepper
sprinkle	paprika
1 cup	Parmesan cheese, grated

Steam rice until just tender. Cook zucchini until just tender.

Mix rice and zucchini with the next seven ingredients. Salt and Pepper to taste. Turn into a greased baking dish approximately 11 x 8 x 2. Dust top with paprika and Parmesan cheese. Bake at 350 degrees for about 1 hour or until firm and light brown. Let cool completely and cut into squares.

Uova al Diavolo
(Deviled Eggs)

6	hard cooked eggs, cut in half
¼ cup	mayonnaise
1½ tablespoons	Parmesan cheese, grated
½ teaspoon	dried oregano leaves, crushed
⅛ teaspoons	garlic powder
6	cherry tomatoes, sliced (optional)

Mash yolks with fork. Blend in remaining ingredients except tomato slices. Refill whites using about 1 tablespoon yolk mixture for each egg half. Garnish with tomato slices if desired.

CHI HA PROVATO IL MALE,
GUSTA MEGLIO IL BENE
He who has tried the worst, appreciates the best

Pesce

(Fish)

Baccalà in Umido
(Codfish in Tomato Sauce)

Borgo a Mozzano (my father's home town) is sister city to a Scandinavian city which is a principal source of Codfish (Baccalà). During the Middle Ages, the poor ate Baccalà during Lent. When John Cabot (Giovanni Caboto) returned to Italy he told of the plentitude of Codfish off the coasts of North America.

whole	codfish (baccalà), soaked
4 or 5 tablespoons	olive oil
1 clove	garlic, minced
1 small	onion chopped or
	4 green onions with tops
	cut into ½ inch pieces
½ cup	parsley, minced
1 tablespoon	dried rosemary
28 ounce can	solid pack tomatoes, chopped
	(juice reserved)
¼ teaspoon	black pepper
¼ cup	chicken bouillon, hot
to taste	salt (optional)

Cut drained and dried codfish into serving pieces. In a skillet heat olive oil, add garlic and fry slowly for 5 minutes, then add onions and cook another 5 minutes. Add parsley, rosemary, and chopped tomatoes with their juice. Cook 10 minutes, then add codfish and black pepper, spooning liquid over the fish. Add no salt. Cover and cook 1 hour, basting fish several times with the sauce. As it cooks down, add a little hot chicken bouillon. When fish is tender add salt if desired. Serve with polenta.

Baccalà alla Fiorentina (Fried Dried Codfish)

1	dried codfish
½ cup	flour
½ cup	olive oil
1 clove	garlic, peeled
to taste	salt

Buy a dried codfish. Soak it in water for at least 12 hours. Drain, dry, and cut in pieces about one inch wide. Dredge in flour. Put olive oil to cover bottom of frying pan with one clove of garlic. Fry until lightly brown on all sides. Sprinkle with a little salt, not too much because soaked baccala is already salted. Serve with mashed potatoes.

Cacciucco (Fish Stew)

---

2 pounds	sole fillet
2 pounds	halibut fillet
¼ cup	olive oil
1	onion, chopped
1 clove	garlic, crushed
½ cup	parsley, chopped
4	tomatoes, peeled and chopped
to taste	salt and pepper
½	lemon, juiced
6 slices	French bread, toasted

Buy approximately 4 slices of both sole and halibut fillets. Wash and dry fish with paper towels. Cut into squares and set aside. Pour olive oil to cover the bottom of a heavy skillet in a thin layer. Fry onion until limp with garlic and parsley. Add tomatoes, salt, and pepper. When the tomatoes are limp (about 20 minutes) add the juice of ½ lemon. Boil a few minutes longer and then pass through a sieve. Return the strained sauce to the pan and add fish and simmer for 30 minutes or until tender. Serve the fish on a heated dish with the sauce poured over it. Serve with toasted French bread to soak up the sauce.

Calamari in Umido (Squid in Mushroom Sauce)

Instructions for cleaning squid:

1. Cut head off below eye level.
2. Disjoint head portion from body and discard.
3. Clean body by removing outside skin.
4. Split body down one side with razor blade and remove bone in center and other material.
5. Wash thoroughly.

MUSHROOM SAUCE:
For ½ **pound** of cleaned **Calamari** use:

2 tablespoons	**olive oil**
2 large	**mushrooms, sliced**
1	**green onion, thinly sliced**
½ clove	**garlic, chopped**
1	**tomato, peeled and diced**
4 sprigs	**parsley, finely chopped**
1 ounce	**sherry wine**
½ ounce	**lemon juice**
to taste	**salt**

Heat olive oil in saute pan; add mushrooms and onions; cook until onions are limp. Add squid, garlic, tomato, and parsley. Reduce heat and cook 3 to 5 minutes. Drain oil from pan. Turn up heat and add sherry. Add lemon juice and simmer for an additional 2 minutes. Serve on a bed of rice.

Calamari Fritti con Salsa (Fried Squid with Sauce)

Put cleaned squid in colander and allow to drain. (See preceeding recipe for cleaning instructions.)

For each ½ **pound** of **Calamari,** make a mixture of:

2	**eggs, separated with whites stiffly beaten**
1 tablespoon	**olive oil**
¾ cup	**beer**
1 cup	**flour, sifted**

Beat egg yolks with beer. Add oil, then add flour. While beating fold in stiffly beaten egg white. Cover mixture with a towel and leave at room temperature about ½ hour.

Dip one squid at a time into mixture to coat. Put each squid in deep hot oil. Fry no longer than 3 minutes. Put drained squid in a flat serving plate.

TOMATO SAUCE:

1-8 ounce can	**tomato sauce**
½ cup	**parsley, minced**
to taste	**salt and pepper**
2 cloves	**garlic, finely chopped**

Mix thoroughly and place in a small bowl in center of serving plate surrounded by prepared squid.

Cannelloni Ripieni di Pesce (Stuffed Seafood Cannelloni)

CREPES:

6	eggs
1 cup	milk
1 cup	flour
2 tablespoons	butter, melted
¼ teaspoon	salt

FILLING:

½	onion, chopped
1 clove	garlic, chopped
½ pound	mushrooms, sliced
1 tablespoon	white wine
1 cup	mozzarella cheese, grated
½ pound	crab meat
½ pound	shrimp
	Sofritto (see page 145)
½ cup	Parmesan cheese, grated

Cannelloni are crepes. To make crepes, beat eggs and milk. Stir in flour and butter. Add salt and blend until smooth. Lightly grease a pan and cook above batter for 1 minute of each side. Set aside on dish with a sheet of wax paper between each crepe.

Prepare filling. Saute onion, garlic and mushrooms and then add white wine, mozzarella cheese, crab meat, and shrimp meat. Gently stir all ingredients. Put by tablespoon on shell and roll.

Place in baking pan and cover all with Sofritto and Parmesan cheese. Put in oven a few minutes at 350 degrees. The cannelloni are ready to serve when the cheese topping is melted.

Cioppino in Umido (Crab Stew)

1 clove	garlic, chopped
½ cup	olive oil
1 tablespoon	butter
1 large	onion, chopped
2 large	crabs, raw and disjointed by fishmonger
½ cup	fresh parsley, minced
1 cup	sherry wine
2 cups	tomatoes, crushed

Fry garlic in olive oil and butter until golden brown. When it starts to color add onion and cook until limp. Add crabs. Toss and keep stirring over a high flame being careful not to burn the garlic and onion for about 5 minutes. Add parsley and sherry wine and cover, continuing to cook over high heat for about 2 to 3 minutes. Add tomatoes, reduce heat to simmer, cover, and continue cooking for another 20 minutes.

Walls of Lucca

Cioppino di Egildo
(Crab Stew Egildo's Style)

Fish Stew, originally a recipe from Corsica given me by my maternal Grandfather Egildo Franceschi.

2 pounds	white fish (halibut) cut in pieces
3 pounds	clams
1	onion, chopped
½ cup	olive oil
½ cube	butter
1 large	crab, raw and disjointed by fishmonger
½ cup	white wine
½ cup	fresh parsley, chopped
1 clove	garlic, minced
1 cup	tomatoes, crushed
½ pound	prawns
½	cabbage, chopped
to taste	light salt
to taste	pepper

Flour and fry white fish a few minutes so that it holds together. Steam clams and reserve the liquid. Fry onion in oil and butter. When limp add crab and saute for a few minutes. Add wine and cook until wine is evaporated. Add parsley and garlic and cook for about

3 minutes. Add tomatoes and cook another 15 minutes. Add white fish, prawns, and cabbage and cook another 5 minutes. Lastly add steamed clams and cook another 10 minutes. Add salt lightly; cioppino makes its own salt. Altogether preparation takes about 1 hour.

NOTE: Liquid may be added any time (from clams) if cioppino seems too dry. If more liquid is needed add broth which has been made from fish or chicken bouillon cubes. Cioppino should be in liquid almost like a soup, but remember that all the fish makes water itself. Serve over french bread slices which have been toasted.

The Italians preach the merits of cabbage. Cabbage is a good source of Vitamin C.

CHI PARLA POCO, BASTA LA META DEL
CERVELLO
He who talks little, only needs half a brain

Conchiglie
(Grilled Scallops)

4	scallops
2 tablespoons	butter
½	onion, chopped
½ cup	fresh parsley, chopped
1 clove	garlic, crushed
to taste	salt and pepper

Grill scallops under a broiler for 5 to 10 minutes. Do not overcook. Slice thin and mix with butter, onion, parsley and garlic. Season with salt and pepper and reheat gently for 2 minutes.

Parsley

Gamberi con Marsala (Prawns with Marsala)

1 pound	jumbo prawns
2 tablespoons	olive oil
1	green onion, chopped
1 clove	garlic, chopped
1	white onion, chopped
½ cup	Marsala wine
½ cup	chicken broth
to taste	salt and pepper

Peel jumbo prawns, remove vein from back and butterfly. Saute prawns in hot oil. Immediately add green onion, garlic, white onion, Marsala, chicken broth, salt and pepper. Simmer 10 minutes. Serve with rice.

Granchio Toscano
(Tuscany Crab)

---

2 tablespoons	butter
1	green pepper, chopped
1 cup	mushrooms, sliced
1 tablespoon	onion, chopped
1 tablespoon	fresh parsley, minced
2 tablespoons	flour
1¾ cups	milk
2	egg yolks, beaten
½ teaspoon	dried thyme
¼ cup	sweet sherry wine
½ teaspoon	dried oregano
to taste	salt and pepper
3 cups	crab meat

Melt butter in saucepan. Add green pepper, mush-rooms, onion, and parsley. Cover and cook slowly for 10 minutes. Blend in flour, milk, and egg and continue cooking, stirring constantly and gently until mixture thickens. Add all other ingredients and heat. Serve on toasted French bread.

My father had seven brothers and sisters. He, his sister, Caterina Sargentini, and his brothers, Silvio and Arturo, came to America in the early 1900s. Their uncle, Danielle Giovannini, was already here and had a restaurant in Occidental, California.

My father's sister, Caterina, married Olivo Sargentini who owned the New Pisa Restaurant (now Basta Pasta) at Vallejo and Grant Avenue. They had two daughters. The first was Gloria, who died and in turn left two daughters: Lorine, who married Leo D'Agostino and is manager of Wells Fargo Bank on Columbus Ave. in North Beach, and Lisa Muschi. The second daughter, Lola, married John Manzella and they own Manzella's Loft in Hayward (across the Bay Bridge). Lola and John had one daughter, Janet, who married Tony Bartholomew.

My father's brother, Arturo, had a real drinking problem and would sit on our front door stoop singing risqué Italian songs. Arturo was a chef and the heat of the stoves "drove him to drink" or so he said. Arturo decided to return to Italy after the Second World War and my father, Caterina, and Silvio forgot to tell him to renew his papers, so he never could return to San Francisco.

My father's brother, Silvio, was my favorite uncle and therein would lie a subject for another book. Silvio married once, a beautiful model named Lillian Nygaard. Lillian died during the Second World War while Silvio was an Air Force Chef in England (his Air Force acquaintances included Clark Gable and Glen Miller).

Silvio and Lillian had one daughter, Linda. Lillian died and Linda was raised by Caterina and Olivo Sargentini so Silvio was a "bachelor uncle." The first time I saw Linda she was in a clothes basket in the living room. Her mother and mine were having coffee in the kitchen while I, at ten years, wanted to hold on to center stage and proceeded to operate on Linda with a pair of scissors. Fortunately they stopped me!! Silvio later worked for the Fior D'Italia Restaurant (Stockton and Union Streets). His free hours he spent either at our house or at the race track at Bay Meadows.

Joseph and Silvio would go fishing every week, many times for catfish in the San Joaquin River, other times for stripe bass in San Francisco Bay's then crystal clear waters. They were once on Wide World of Sports, an ABC special, and my father won numerous sports awards for fishing and bocce ball tournaments.

One particular day, they came sulking home for lunch. Silvio had his hand over his eye. My mother kept asking what was wrong but no one answered. Finally, the truth . . . my father had tied a sack of catfish to the side of the boat. The next catch he told Silvio to put more fish in the sack. Somehow the sack slipped to the bottom of the San Joaquin River, at which point my father not only threw Silvio overboard, "Go get the fish," but also gave him a "bell'occhio nero" (a black eye).

Here's the recipe for those darn catfish that didn't get away. . . .

Pesce Gatto con Bietola (Catfish with Swiss Chard)

1 clove	garlic, chopped
1 medium size	onion, chopped
½ cup	olive oil
2 tablespoons	butter
1 sprig	fresh rosemary, removed from stalks and chopped
3 leaves	fresh sage, chopped
½ cup	parsley, chopped
2 cups	solid pack tomatoes, crushed
1 bunch	Swiss chard, cut in strips
3 or 4	catfish, cleaned
to taste	salt and pepper
2 cups	fish broth

Fry garlic and onion in olive oil and butter until soft. When it begins to turn gold add herbs and parsley. Fry a few more minutes. Add tomatoes and Swiss chard. Don't chop Swiss chard too thin but rather cut in strips. Use stalks of chard too. Let mixture cook for ½ hour then add whole fish, placing on top of sauce, neat and even. Sprinkle with salt and pepper on top of fish. Add fish broth. Bake in oven until done, about 40 minutes. Baste occasionally with its own sauce.

Pesce con Pancetta, Capperi e Limone (Snapper with Italian Bacon, Capers and Lemon)

½ cup	flour
two 6-8 ounce	Pacific red snapper fillets
3 ounces	olive oil
1 teaspoon	garlic, minced
⅓ pound	pancetta, diced
2 ounces	white wine
2 tablespoons	capers
2 tablespoons	lemon juice, freshly squeezed
3 ounces	fish stock, clam juice or water
to taste	salt and pepper
2 tablespoons	parsley, chopped

Lightly flour the snapper fillets and heat a 10 inch frying pan until very hot. Add 2 ounces of olive oil and saute each side of the fillet for 3-4 minutes or until well done. Remove the cooked snapper fillets to 2 serving plates and keep warm.

Add the remaining olive oil to the same pan and saute the garlic and pancetta lightly. Add the white wine, capers, lemon juice, and stock. Reduce it by half on high heat. Season with salt and pepper. Add the chopped parsley, mix well and spoon sauce equally over the snapper fillets and serve immediately.

Ostriche Gratinate (Stuffed Oysters on the Half Shell)

Oysters are preferred raw and alive. If open, do not buy. They are then split leaving as much liquid as possible on the half shell.

12 oysters, on half shell

MIXTURE:

12 tablespoons	parsley, chopped
1 stalk	celery, finely chopped
6 cloves	garlic, finely chopped
6 teaspoons	dried thyme
to taste	pepper
12 tablespoons	breadcrumbs
¼ cup	olive oil
2	lemons, juiced

Combine mixture thoroughly. Put one tablespoon of mixture on top of each oyster. Sprinkle with a few drops of olive oil and broil for 3 minutes. Remove from broiler and squeeze 5 drops of lemon juice on each oyster.

Scampi alla Crema (Creamed Shrimp)

1 teaspoon	shallots, minced
2 tablespoons	butter
to taste	salt
to taste	white pepper
32	shrimp, butterflied
½ cup	dry white wine
½ cup	heavy cream

Lightly saute shallots in butter. Add salted and peppered shrimp and saute for 2 minutes. Add wine, bring to boil and remove shrimp. Add cream, stir, and let sauce reduce over high heat to two-thirds. Reheat shrimp in the sauce and serve immediately.

Sogliola Viareggio (Sole Viareggio)

1	onion, chopped
1 clove	garlic, minced
¼ cup	olive oil
1 tablespoon	fresh oregano
½ cup	white wine
1 cup	tomatoes, crushed
1-8 ounce can	tomato sauce
1 cup	water
2 pounds	fillet of sole
½ pound	mushrooms, sliced
1 bunch	spinach, boiled and chopped
to taste	salt and pepper

Saute onion and garlic in olive oil until onion becomes limp. Add oregano, white wine, tomatoes, tomato sauce, and water. Cook this sauce for 5 minutes. Add fillet of sole and mushrooms. Cook over low heat for 15 minutes. A few minutes before fish is cooked add spinach. Season with salt and pepper.

Sugo di Pesce
(Fish Sauce)

Mushrooms will not dry if poisonous. Dried mushrooms from the Sierras and Shasta are a good substitute. (California's Rossi brand is very popular here).

1 tablespoon	olive oil
1	onion, chopped
½ cube	butter
1 tablespoon	flour
2 tablespoons	white wine
1 cup	water or fish stock
1 tablespoon	tomato sauce
½ ounce	dried porcini mushrooms, reconstituted, chopped
2	anchovies, minced
1 tablespoon	parsley, chopped
1 sprig	rosemary, removed from stalks and chopped
to taste	salt and pepper

Heat the oil and brown the onion. Add butter and stir in flour. Slowly add wine, water (or fish stock) and tomato sauce stirring all the time to make sure the mixture doesn't stick to the bottom of the pan. Add mushrooms, anchovies and remaining seasonings. Cook together for 10 minutes then pass through a sieve and use as directed above when cooking trout, etc. It is also good with shell fish dishes.

Tartara
(Tartar Sauce)

1 cup	mayonnaise
1½ tablespoons	sweet pickle relish
1	green onion, chopped
1 teaspoon	lemon juice

Combine all ingredients. Refrigerate until ready to use.

PARLARE SENZA PENSARE,
È COME SPARARE SENZA MIRARE
To talk without thinking is like
shooting without aiming

Zuppa di Gamberi (Prawn Soup)

24	prawns
4 quarts	water
2	onions, 1 whole and 1 chopped
2 cloves	garlic, whole
1-8 ounce glass	white wine
2	fish bouillon cubes
1	leek, white part only, chopped
2 ounces	dried procini mushrooms, reconstituted and chopped
¼ cup	olive oil
1-8 ounce can	tomato sauce
to taste	salt and pepper

Peel prawns and put shells in water with whole onion, 1 clove of garlic, wine, and 1½ cups of broth made with 1 bouillon cube. Cook for 1 hour, strain through a colander.

In a large saucepan add chopped onion, the remaining clove of garlic, leek, and mushrooms. Saute these ingredients in olive oil. Add prawns, the remaining bouillon cube and the tomato sauce. Add to strained broth and bring to a slow boil. Boil 25 minutes adding salt and pepper to taste. Serve with croutons.

Primi

(Soup, Pasta, Polenta and Rice)

The first course is usually a dish of Soup, Pasta, Rice, or Polenta. Literally, it is not the first course since we've usually already had our antipasto or fish plate.

We have three sons. The first, Peter, had never finished a complete meal. I don't think I can honestly say my son ever sat down and let us eat in peace or, for that matter, he never finished a complete bottle of milk during his early days. As he grew up, every time we would sit at the table we would have to hear moaning and groaning. In most Italian families children are not allowed to eat before the family. It is thought that a family must eat together, no matter what consequences a mother must suffer. At any rate, we would no sooner be seated when the moaning would start, "Meeee noooo like . . ." His best excuse when he didn't want to eat was, "Meeee ate scrambled eggs this morningggg . . ." This scrambled eggs bit always seemed to hit his father in his weakest spot, the head. Well, after having tried everything in the book including the Italian Pepper Up, Ferrochina Bisleri, I decided this has got to stop!! We got off on our new road in this way. MONDAY . . . got up, started eating breakfast, didn't want, didn't get. Lunchtime, "Meeee ate scrambled eggs this morningg . . . didn't want't lunch, didn't get . . . MONDAY NIGHT, stayed awake until two a.m., wanted dinner, didn't get . . . TUESDAY, same routine. WEDNESDAY, hunger is starting to set in, pretty good breakfast, lousy lunch, little dinner. THURSDAY, started thinking, "these people don't give a damn whether I eat or not, I'd better start digging in." GOOD BREAKFAST, GOOD LUNCH, GOOD DINNER . . . FRIDAY, ate everything on breakfast plate, ate everything on lunch plate, ate everything on dinner plate. The result of this experiment was a gain of three pounds in two months.

Minestre

(Soups)

Briciolata (Crumb Soup)

1 pound	salad macaroni, boiled and drained
1 cup	olive oil
3 tablespoons	bread crumbs
to taste	salt and ground black pepper

Keep salad macaroni warm.

Heat olive oil in a saucepan over low flame. When oil is hot, add bread crumbs and salt. Saute gently until bread crumbs are golden brown, then remove pan from heat and sprinkle with salt and pepper. Pour above mixture over macaroni and mix thoroughly. Serve immediately. Do not add any cheese.

My maternal uncle, Claude, who was Richard Franceschi's father owned the Barbary Restaurant at Pacific and Montgomery Streets. He had a number of wives. In between wives, he lived in a penthouse apartment on Greenwich Street at the foot of the Telegraph Hill steps. Being his only available niece, I had to go up there after school to clean his apartment and, on Saturdays, make broth for the week. During that time he married Katherine McDermott (I lost her number in line) who was the daughter of the Business Manager for the Hearst newspapers. That marriage lasted until Katherine died. She would let me and my girlfriends have parties at their Telegraph Hill penthouse apartment. On one particular occasion, the City of San Francisco lost its Telegraph Hill bus and the driver. He had parked the bus on a side street and had come to our party. Claude and Katherine had a lawyer friend (Melvin Belli). I remember how thrilled I was to attend my first "society" wedding when they took me to Melvin Belli's wedding at Belli's Telegraph Hill apartment.

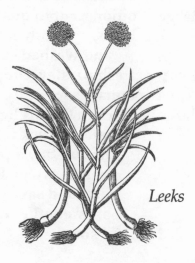

Leeks

Brodo di Gallina (Chicken Broth)

Chicken broth is the base for many Italian soups and risotto and is used in many recipes to lengthen the sauce. In our house broth is made about twice a month. It is a lengthy process but during the 35 years that I worked it was nice to be able to come home, take a container of broth out of the freezer, thaw it, add tortellini or pastina and serve it. This particular recipe was made on a 1 burner electric plate and served on October 19, 1989 when power was restored after the earthquake in the Marina District.

8 quarts	water
1	parsnip, peeled and quartered
2	turnips, peeled and quartered
2 cloves	garlic
4 stalks	celery, cut in two inch pieces
5	carrots, cut in 2 inch pieces
2 large	onions, cut in quarters
2	leeks, split down the middle and washed carefully
1 cup	fresh parsley, chopped
2-8 ounce cans	tomato sauce
1 large	chicken (hen is best)
½	boneless chuck roast. (if you buy a packaged boneless chuck roast use half and save half for making stew another night)
1	beef shank

> 1   veal shank
> to taste   salt and pepper

Take a very large pot (about 10 quarts) and fill with water. Put in parsnip, turnips, garlic, celery, carrots, onions, leeks, parsley, and tomato sauce. Bring to a rolling boil. Add chicken which has been washed and cleaned inside but left whole, chuck roast, beef shank, and veal shank. Bring back to a slow boil. Boil 2 hours, remove the chicken and the meats. If using a hen, boil 2½ hours and then remove the chicken and the meat. Keep the vegetables you want to eat in a separate dish, then strain broth through a colander. Let cool, preferably overnight. Cut meat and chicken in pieces, put on a large platter. Serve with a jar of pickles, Peperoncini sauce, mustard, or catsup. When broth is strained and cooled, put in refrigerator in jars or in plastic containers in freezer.

One good way to serve the broth is to bring it to a boil and add 1 package of tortellini, following directions on package, but that is a meal in itself.

Crocchette
(Minced Meat Patties)

If you don't care to eat the plain boiled meats, you might try this recipe for minced meat patties. I usually make the broth Saturday or Sunday and Crocchette Monday night.

3 large cloves	garlic, finely chopped
4	onions, finely chopped
left over	chicken and meats from recipe for Chicken Broth, page 94
½ cup	Parmesan cheese, grated
6	eggs, well beaten
4 tablespoons	parsley, chopped
3 sprigs	rosemary, removed from stalks and chopped
6 leaves	fresh sage, chopped
1 tablespoon	dried thyme leaves
to taste	salt and pepper
½ cup	flour
½ cup	olive oil

Fry garlic and onions in olive oil until onions are limp. Discard skin from chicken and finely chop chicken. Remove beef from any bones, chop fine. Place all ingredients in a large bowl. Add Parmesan cheese, eggs, parsley, rosemary, sage, thyme leaves, and salt and pepper. Mix all ingredients well. Put flour in a pie plate. Take an ice cream scoop full of meat and press onto flour, then turn patty to coat other side with flour.

Put olive oil in frying pan and fry crocchettas over medium heat 5 minutes on one side, turn and 5 minutes on other side. Remove from heat, keep warm and serve with your favorite vegetable.

A Tuscan meat market

Brodo di Manzo
(Beef Broth)

2 pieces	beef short ribs
4 stalks	celery, cut in pieces
4	carrots, cut in pieces
1	onion, quartered
2 cloves	garlic
5 quarts	water
2 tablespoons	salt
2 teaspoons	pepper, coarsely ground
1-8 ounce can	tomato sauce
½ cup	fresh parsley, chopped

Place meat, celery, carrots, onion and garlic in boiling water. When water returns to boil, add salt, pepper, tomato sauce, and parsley. Boil for approximately 2 hours or until meat is tender. Serve meat with Peperoncini sauce. Serve broth with either toasted French bread or soup paste. Top all with Parmesan cheese.

After you have drained off meat and vegetables, broth can also be used when recipe calls for a beef base.

PEPERONCINI SAUCE:

6	peperoncini, chopped
1	onion, chopped
½ cup	olive oil
¼ cup	Parmesan cheese, grated

Broglio Castle where Chianti Wine is made

Torre Del Lago Puccini

Crema di Pomodori
(Cream of Tomato Soup)

A large quantity recipe to feed a crowd.

1 pound	onions, diced
1 pound	celery, diced
1 pound	carrots, diced
½ cup	olive oil
2-#10 cans	tomatoes, crushed
2 quarts	stock or water
1	bay leaf
⅓ cup	sugar
2 teaspoons	baking soda
½ gallon	cream sauce (recipe follows)

Saute vegetables in oil in heavy soup pot until onions are transparent. Add all tomato products, stock or water, bay leaf and sugar. Simmer 1½ to 2 hours.

Remove from heat. Add baking soda and blend well.

CREAM SAUCE:

1 cube	butter
1 cup	flour
½ gallon	milk

Heat to boiling point.

Add cream sauce to soup gradually, blending well. Should be consistency of heavy cream. Reheat slowly, excessive heat may cause soup to curdle.

Minestra dei Bimbi (Baby Soup)

1 quart	milk
1-6 ounce package	pastina
1 teaspoon	salt
2 tablespoons	sugar
1	egg, beaten
2 tablespoons	butter, melted
4 or 5 sprigs	parsley, finely chopped

Heat milk until it reaches boiling point, then start adding pastina (see note). Add salt and sugar. Let boil for 10 minutes; remove from heat. Beat egg and butter together for about 2 minutes. Add to boiled mixture and stir well. Sprinkle with parsley.

NOTE: Pastina is tiny pasta which may be purchased in an Italian delicatessen.

Minestra della Mamma Gemma (My Mother Gemma's Vegetable Rice Soup)

1-28 ounce can	solid pack tomatoes
1	potato, cubed
2 tablespoons	butter
1 stalk	celery, chopped
1	carrot, cubed
1	leek, sliced
1 small	onion, chopped
8 cups	water
to taste	salt and pepper
1 clove	garlic, minced
1 cup	rice

In a large pot combine tomatoes, potato, butter, celery, carrot, leek, onion, water, salt, pepper, and garlic. When vegetables are tender add rice and boil until rice is tender, about 20 minutes.

Minestra di Castagne (Chestnut Soup)

8 ounces	fresh chestnuts
4 cups	chicken broth
1 slice	lean ham
1	bay leaf
2	cloves, whole

Score the chestnuts across the pointed end and bake in a moderate oven for 10 to 15 minutes at which time the outer and inner skins should easily peel away. Take peeled chestnuts and cook slowly in the chicken broth with ham and seasonings for about 1 hour. Pass through a sieve and serve with Fried Bread. (See page 53).

Chestnut

Minestra di Coda di Bue (Oxtail Soup)

1 cube	butter
¼ pound	prosciutto, cubed
5 quarts	water
2 pounds	lean beef
2	oxtails, cut in sections by butcher
2 tablespoons	salt
1 teaspoon	black pepper
2	bay leaves
2 tablespoons	Worcestershire sauce
1 tablespoon each	dried thyme and marjoram
6 leaves	basil, chopped
3 sprigs	parsley, chopped
1-8 ounce can	tomato sauce
¼ cup	olive oil
5 cloves	garlic, chopped
4 large	onions, cut into small pieces
3	turnips, peeled and cut into small pieces
6 stalks	celery, chopped
6	carrots, chopped
4	whole cloves
¾ cup	red wine
2 tablespoons	flour

Melt butter in a skillet. Fry prosciutto in butter and then discard. Add beef and oxtails and fry until well browned. Set aside.

Put 5 quarts water in a large kettle and bring to a boil. Add meats, and the next 8 ingredients and tomato sauce.

In olive oil, saute garlic in frying pan and add remaining vegetables and cloves, frying until vegetables are limp. Remove cloves; add vegetables to soup mixture.

In same skillet, add a cup of soup mixture and wine. Stir in flour, stirring to make a thick paste. Return to soup mixture for thickening.

Let combined ingredients simmer about 2 hours. (Always cover kettles when simmering to avoid evaporation). Before serving, carefully take meat out of pot, remove from bones, and then return to soup.

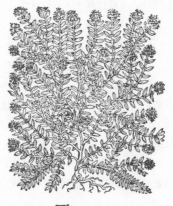

Thyme

Minestra di Fagioli con Salsiccia e Prosciutto (Bean Soup with Sausage and Italian Ham)

1 pound	cranberry beans, dried
1 tablespoon	olive oil
1	onion, chopped
2 cloves	garlic, minced
1 large	green bell pepper, seeded and chopped
1 large	red bell pepper, seeded and chopped
1	carrot, chopped
4 small	leeks, chopped
3 stalks	celery, chopped
1 -14½ ounce can	tomatoes, crushed
4 quarts	chicken broth
½ cup	red wine
1	prosciutto bone or a big chunk of prosciutto
1	bay leaf
6 leaves	fresh basil, minced
1 tablespoon	dried oregano, crushed
6 links	Italian sausages, whole
¼ cup	red wine vinegar
4 ounces	salad macaroni, cooked

In a bowl cover beans with water and let soak overnight. Drain through colander and rinse with water. Set aside. In a 10 quart pot, heat olive oil over medium heat. Add onion and saute until limp about 5 minutes. Add garlic, green and red peppers, carrot, leeks, and celery. Saute 5 more minutes. Add tomatoes with their liquid and simmer another 10 minutes. Add beans, chicken broth, wine, and bone or chunk of prosciutto and bring to boil. Skim surface, add bay leaf, basil, oregano, and Italian sausages. Reduce heat and simmer 2 hours. Add the cooked salad macaroni to soup last, just before serving.

NOTE: Italian Delicatessens will sell the prosciutto bones, sometimes with quite a bit of meat still on it.

Cutting meat in an Italian Delicatessen

Minestra di Pane al Forno (Bread Soup in the Oven)

Religious rules imposed abstinence from meat on Fridays and some of the Orders imposed abstinence six days a week.

When preparing to put soup in oven you might add some fish, cheese, eggs, or frog legs (frogs were not considered meat). Many travelers would ask the hostelers the secret of the soup but the Holy Monks never revealed that they had used CHICKEN BROTH in their soup. They presumably confessed that sin frequently.

6 slices	French bread
½ cup	butter, melted
½ cup	Parmesan cheese, grated
1 quart	chicken broth
to taste	salt and pepper

Take French bread slices and toast them. Spread slices with butter and sprinkle with Parmesan cheese. Take a deep sided baking pan and lay slices evenly across bottom. Slowly pour chicken broth to top of bread, sprinkle again with Parmesan cheese, salt and pepper. Put in a 350 degree oven for about 20 minutes or until bread has absorbed all the liquid. Serve hot.

Minestra di Patate con Quatro Formaggi (Potato Soup with Four Cheeses)

1 cube	unsalted butter
1 large	onion, chopped
8 cups	chicken stock, preferably homemade
2 cups	dry white wine
2 large	boiling potatoes, peeled and diced
1 cup	milk
2 cups	whipping cream
½ cup	mozzarella cheese, shredded
½ cup	fontina cheese, shredded
½ cup	Gorgonzola cheese, crumbled
½ cup	Parmesan cheese, grated
to taste	salt and pepper

In a large pot or Dutch oven, melt butter. Stir in onion and cook until softened, about 10 minutes. Add chicken stock, wine and potatoes and simmer, uncovered, until potatoes are tender, about 25 minutes. Stir in milk and whipping cream and then puree with a hand mixer directly on stove. Continue to heat over medium low heat. Add cheeses, stirring frequently until cheeses are completely melted. Season with salt and pepper.

Minestra di Pesce (Fish Soup)

2 pounds	any fish, including heads and tails
1	bay leaf
6	peppercorns
½ cup	fresh parsley, chopped
2 quarts	water
1 cup	white wine
2 tablespoons	butter
1	onion, chopped
4	tomatoes, peeled and chopped
1 stalk	celery, chopped
to taste	salt and pepper
1 pound	shell fish
2 pound	mussels, cleaned

Take whole fish; remove head and tail and boil with bay leaf, peppercorns, parsley, water and wine for 10 minutes. Strain and keep liquid. Melt butter in large saucepan, add onion and fry until golden. Add tomatoes, celery, and salt and pepper; bring to a boil. Add reserved stock; reheat; add body of fish cut in large pieces, shell fish and mussels. Boil another 20 minutes and serve.

Minestra di Porri
(Leek and Potato Soup)

4	leeks
1	onion, sliced thin
5 tablespoons	butter
7 cups	chicken or beef stock, hot
to taste	salt and pepper
4	potatoes, peeled and thinly sliced

Thoroughly clean leeks, split and slice thin. Add onion and 3 tablespooons of butter, cook slowly over a low fire until limp but not brown. Add chicken or beef stock and salt and pepper if needed. Bring to a boil. Cover, lower the heat and allow to simmer half an hour. Add potatoes to soup, cover, and simmer until the potatoes are very tender. Taste again for seasoning. Before serving, remove the soup from the fire and stir in the remaining 2 tablespoons of butter.

Minestra di Riso e Spinaci (Rice and Spinach Soup)

1 pound	spinach, washed thoroughly
2 cloves	garlic, minced
6 tablespoons	butter
2	onions, chopped
8 cups	chicken broth
1 cup	rice, uncooked
to taste	salt and pepper
¼ pound	Parmesan cheese, grated

Boil spinach just until limp, about 1 minute. Drain. Chop coarsely.

Heat butter in a 6 quart saucepan. Add garlic and onion and saute over medium heat until soft. Add spinach and stir. Add chicken broth and bring to a boil. Add rice and boil slowly about 20 minutes or until tender. Season with salt and pepper. Serve soup in bowl and sprinkle with Parmesan cheese.

Stracciatella (Broth with Eggs and Cheese)

2	eggs
⅓ cup	Parmesan cheese, grated
½ cup	parsley flakes
1 teaspoon	ground nutmeg
½ cup	Romano cheese
4 cups	water
6	chicken bouillon cubes
¼ cup	bread crumbs

In small bowl, beat eggs lightly with Parmesan cheese, parsley flakes, nutmeg and Romano cheese.

In medium saucepan, bring water to a boil; add bouillon; boil 5 more minutes. Remove from heat, add cheese mixture and stir to blend well. Sprinkle with bread crumbs, stirring until mixed. Let stand 1 minute. Serve with extra Parmesan cheese, if desired.

Beans, pasta, rice, and polenta sold from sacks in Italian markets.

OGNI MONTE HA LA SUA VALLE
Each mountain has its own valley

Pasta

(Various Noodles)

Cannelloni (Pasta Tubes for Various Fillings)

For Cannelloni use Pasta recipe (page 130). When pasta has had its final rolling, cut into oblongs about 4 inches by 3 inches. Spread with one of the meat, cheese, chicken, or spinach Ravioli fillings, roll, place in a pan, and cover with your favorite sauce and heat in the oven before serving.

CHI CAMMINA CON GLI SOPPI ANDRÀ ZOPPO
He who travels with cripples will soon limp

Cannelloni con Granchio e Spinaci (Crab and Spinach Filling for Cannelloni)

Make Cannelloni pasta according to previous recipe or buy prepared shells and prepare according to package directions.

6 to 8 ounces	crab meat
1-10 ounce box	frozen spinach
1 clove	garlic, mashed
2 tablespoons	butter
1½ cups	ricotta cheese
½ cup	Parmesan cheese, grated
½ cup	green onion, minced
1	egg
to taste	salt

Shred crab. Cook spinach according to package directions, drain thoroughly. Saute spinach and garlic in butter for 5 minutes, combine with cheeses, green onions, egg, crab, and salt. Mix well. Spread filling along the center of each pasta rectangle and roll up or fill shells with filling if using purchased shells. Top with Parmesan Sauce. Bake in 425 degree oven for 20 to 25 minutes.

PARMESAN SAUCE:

½ cube	butter
½ cup	flour
½ cup	milk
¼ cup	whipping cream
½ cup	Parmesan cheese, grated
to taste	salt

Melt butter in a saucepan, blend in flour. Gradually add milk and cream, cook and stir until thickened and bubbly. Add cheese and salt to taste, heat and stir until cheese is melted.

Cheese displayed in window

Conchiglie Piene
(Beef Stuffed Shells)

Buy one pound of huge packaged shells (aka con-chiglie). Parboil in four quarts of salted water approximately 7 minutes or until just tender. Drain and cool.

BEEF FILLING:

2 tablespoons	olive oil
2 tablespoons	butter
1 small	onion, chopped
1 clove	garlic, minced
¼ teaspoon	dried oregano
1½ pounds	ground beef
1	egg, slightly beaten
to taste	salt and pepper
3 slices	bread, soaked in milk
½ pound	mozzarella cheese, grated

Heat oil and butter in skillet. Add onion, garlic and oregano to skillet, cooking until limp. Add ground beef and cook 10 minutes, stirring well. Add egg, salt and pepper, drained soaked bread, and mozzarella cheese. With a small spoon, fill cooked shells and place them in a buttered baking dish. Spoon your favorite tomato or meat sauce and additional mozzarella cheese over top. Bake 25 to 30 minutes or until bubbly.

The filling may also be used as stuffing for Manicotti, long tubular pasta.

Fettuccine
(Ribbon Shaped Noodles)

1 pound	fettuccine noodles, packaged
2 cups	whipping cream
2	egg yolks
2 teaspoons	fresh parsley, finely chopped
1 cup	Parmesan cheese, grated
½ cube	unsalted butter
1 teaspoon	whole nutmeg, grated
to taste	salt and pepper
2 tablespoons	additional butter
½ pound	mushrooms, thinly sliced

Cook fettuccine until al dente (firm) in salted, boiling water. Drain in a colander, rinse with cold water and set aside.

Mix cream and egg yolks until well combined but do not over mix. Place cream-egg yolk mixture in a large saucepan and add parsley, cheese, butter, nutmeg, salt and pepper. Bring mixture to a simmer over low heat, stirring constantly. Do not boil or cream will curdle. Let simmer until creamy and rather thick about 2 minutes. Add fettuccine to saucepan, turning and lifting until pasta is hot and coated with sauce. Garnish with mushrooms which have been sauteed in butter separately.

Gnocchi ("Knock on Wood" Potato Dumplings)

6 cups	flour
3 cups	potatoes, boiled
2 tablespoons	olive oil
1	egg
to taste	butter
to taste	your favorite sauce

Remove skin and mash potatoes; pass through sieve while potatoes are hot. Sift flour and form a well on dough board. Immediately place potatoes and oil inside well.

Turn potato dough out onto a well floured board and knead gently about 20 times. Shape into a loaf and set on a floured area to prevent sticking.

Cut loaf into four pieces. Roll piece into a cord about ½ inch thick. Cut cord in 1 inch lengths. Roll each piece on the back of a fork to give it ridges. Set each piece on a lightly floured pan such as a baking sheet leaving space between each one. You now have gnocchi. When all the pieces have been made put in freezer (still in pan) for about 2 hours. When hard put in a plastic bag and these will keep for about 2 months.

When ready to cook bring about 3 quarts of water to a boil. Add oil and salt to water. Drop frozen gnocchi into water a few at a time. As soon as they pop to surface remove with a slotted spoon, put in a dish with rounded sides (pasta bowl). Add butter and sprinkle with Parmesan cheese or serve with your favorite meat or pesto sauce.

Walls of Lucca

*Joseph's
first
communion
table*

When my son Joseph Enrico received his First Holy Communion, we hosted a dinner in our garage in the Marina District of San Francisco.

His Godmother and Godfather, Gloria and Ralph Romano, Proprietors of Romano's Restaurant on Lombard Street, insisted on preparing food and serving it on plates that Ralph had just unpacked from Italy for use at the restaurant.

The dedication of this book to their eldest son Robert is a heartfelt thanks for the Romanos and their sons Robert and Richard's many years of friendship.

Ralph Romano died at age 54 from a heart attack. Robert Romano died at age 33.

On those plates a lasagna was first served. This is my version of those lasagnas.

Gloria Romano gave Joseph those plates that are now 20 years old. The restaurant was closed after the 1989 earthquake.

Ralph and Robert, Rest in Peace.

Left to right: Ralph Romano, Joseph Figone, Gloria Romano, Robert Romano at First Communion dinner

Lasagne di Spinaci
(Baked Spinach Lasagne)

1 lb. 12 oz. can	whole tomatoes
1-8 ounce can	tomato sauce
1-6 ounce can	tomato paste
1 cup	onion, chopped
1½ pounds	mushrooms, sliced
2 cloves	garlic, pressed
1 tablespoon	parsley, chopped
6 leaves	fresh basil, chopped
1 teaspoon	dried oregano
to taste	pepper
1-14 ounce carton	ricotta cheese
½ cup	milk
2 bunches, about 1 pound	fresh spinach, or
2-10 ounce boxes	frozen chopped spinach,
8 ounces	packaged lasagna (dough strips), cooked and drained
2 cups	mozzarella cheese, shredded
3 tablespoons	Parmesan cheese, grated

Chop up whole tomatoes; put in saucepan, add tomato sauce and paste, onion, mushrooms, garlic, parsley, basil, oregano and pepper. Bring to a boil, reduce heat and simmer, uncovered, 15 to 20 minutes.

In small bowl combine ricotta, milk, mixing to blend well.

Rinse, trim and coarsely chop spinach, steam briefly to wilt, then dry on toweling. For frozen spinach, thaw and squeeze to drain thoroughly.

To assemble lasagna, coat bottom of 13x9 baking dish with the prepared tomato sauce, then arrange ⅓ of the noodles on top of this sauce. Using ⅓ of each, layer ricotta, cheese, spinach, tomato sauce and mozzarella cheese.

Repeat layering ingredients 2 more times, ending with mozzarella. Sprinkle top with Parmesan cheese. Cover loosely with foil. Bake in a 375 degree oven 30 minutes. Remove foil, bake 5 to 10 minutes longer, until filling is bubbly and cheese is melted. Remove from oven, let stand 10 to 15 minutes before serving.

Joe and his godmother, in black (Gloria Romano today), and her sister, Vera.

Aerial View of Lucca

My father was operating his restaurant, the Universe, on Broadway Street here in San Francisco, when one day, my grandfather, grandmother, and my mother, Gemma, came to San Francisco to visit my grandfather's sister, Filomena Malfatti. They decided to have lunch on Broadway Street. My father thought my mother was cute and wanted to introduce her to his brother Silvio. Sometime later, he and his brother returned the visit by going to Prospect Island where my grandfather was farming at the time. In order to get to the house they had to row across the Delta canals.

My mother didn't care for Silvio but fell in love with my father. The canals were filled with Cattails (Tulli) and for evermore my father referred to my mother as "La Regina Dei Tulli" (the queen of the cattails). He also would laughingly say that "he had brought the Jackass to drink, but that HE had fallen into the river. . . ."

After my mother and father had been married, my uncles Silvio and Arturo lived with them as was the custom at the time, the younger brothers lived with the oldest. When I was born, my parents' first words were, "Oh, my God, she looks just like Silvio!"

Malfatti
(Spinach Balls)

My mother's aunt, Filomena Franceschi, married into the Malfatti family. Her son, Joe, is still in constant contact with my mother. Joe's son, Paul, is a Battalion Chief with the San Francisco Fire Department. The fire department "cooks" in each fire house are a legend of San Francisco cuisine.

4-10 ounce boxes	frozen spinach, chopped
5 or 6	eggs, beaten
1 pound	ricotta cheese
1½ cups	Parmesan cheese, grated
1½ cups	bread crumbs
½ cup	parsley, chopped
1 teaspoon	dried thyme
2 cloves	garlic, minced
1 teaspoon	Italian seasoning
to taste	salt and pepper
as needed	flour

Cook spinach according to directions. Cool, drain and squeeze out liquid. Add eggs, then mix thoroughly with spinach, ricotta, and remainder of ingredients to resemble a meat loaf mixture. Roll in small balls about the size of a large marble. Roll in flour. Place in a floured dish or tray. Sprinkle a little flour on top of balls then put sheet of wax paper on top. Prepare another layer and continue until all mixture is used, sprinkling with flour after each layer. Store in freezer until hard. When ready to serve, boil in salted water 12 to 15 minutes. Drain and mix with your favorite tomato or meat sauce and top with grated Parmesan cheese.

Seated left to right: Robert Figone, brother-in-law; Carlotta Figone, mother-in-law; Aldo Figone, author's husband.
Standing left to right: Christopher Figone, nephew; Gina Figone, niece; Jeffrey Figone, nephew; Liana T. Figone, sister-in-law; Barbara Figone, niece; Frank J. Figone, author's son; Author; Peter J. Figone, author's son; Joseph E. Figone, author's son.

Pasta con Uova (Egg Dough for Various Pastas)

My mother-in-law, Carlotta Figone, tried for years to teach me to make homemade pasta. If you have time to experiment, you may want to try your hand at making pasta for yourself. Remember that cooking time for homemade pasta is less than the cooking time for packaged types. You will need a fairly large pastry board or wood surface and a good wide rolling pin.

6 cups	flour
2 teaspoons	salt
1¼ cups	water (hot from tap)
2	eggs, slightly beaten

Put flour on board making a well in the center. Add salt and eggs and water about a third at a time. Fold the flour over the well ingredients incorporating from inner walls of well, a little at a time until all the flour and water has been used. Knead 10 minutes or until dough is smooth and shiny using additional flour to prevent sticking to board. When you have a fairly solid but soft ball, the consistency is right. Divide dough in half and knead each half another 10 minutes. Put dough under 2 inverted bowls and let rest for at least an hour. Take one of the balls of dough and put in center of floured board. With rolling pin start spreading by rolling pin over back and forth, lifting it, flouring the board, and putting pasta dough down on board, roll in another direction. Continue spreading in various directions turning pasta over from time to time until about ¼ inch thick. Spread a floured cloth over the back of a chair and lay the pasta over it while you proceed similarly with the other half.

FOR NOODLES, SPAGHETTI, ETC:

Let pasta dry for 30 minutes after which roll them up as you would a jelly roll and with a sharp knife cut across the roll at ½ inch widths for noodles, ¼ inch widths for spaghetti. Lay them on a floured cloth until you are ready to cook and remember 5 minutes in boiling salted water for homemade pasta is sufficient.

FOR RAVIOLI:

Roll pasta slightly thinner to about ⅛ inch thickness. Immediately after rolling out both sheets, flour board again, put one sheet down and dot with your favorite filling at ½ inch intervals. Spread a beaten egg in the paths between the dots of filling then gently put second sheet of paste on top. Pass your finger firmly where the paths are. Run a pastry wheel between the fillings so that you have a series of little filled envelopes of pasta. Transfer these to a floured dish being careful not to overlap. Place in freezer until firm. Then you may either use them or put in plastic bags for future use.

Boil ravioli in about 4 quarts of water (for this amount) with salt and oil until they pop to the surface. There are also rolling pins for ravioli (with cut squares and ravioli machines available in hardware stores).

Pasta al Limone (Noodles with Lemon Sauce)

1 pint	whipping cream
½ cube	butter
to taste	salt
1 teaspoon	nutmeg, grated
1 rind of	lemon, finely grated
1 pound	packaged linguine noodles
½ cup	Parmesan cheese, grated

Put whipping cream and butter to heat slowly. Add salt and nutmeg. Simmer to boiling point. Add lemon rind to the above. Bring 1 gallon of water to boiling point, add 2 tablespoons salt. Add linguine and boil 5 minutes. Drain linguine and pour on sauce. Top with Parmesan cheese and toss well.

NOTE: This recipe requires no pepper.

Lemon

Penne Arrabbiate (Penne Noodles with Mad Sauce)

The red peppers make this sauce very hot and spicy. When the chefs are under pressure the waiters will tell them to go and eat some "Penne Arrabbiate."

1 clove	garlic, chopped
1	onion, chopped
½ cup	olive oil
1-28 ounce can	tomatoes (preferably pomodori pelati from Italy), crushed
2	dried red peppers, chopped
1 tablespoon	salt
1 pound	packaged Penne pasta
½ cup	Parmesan cheese, grated

Saute garlic and onion in olive oil. Add tomatoes and red peppers. Simmer until peppers are limp. Bring 1 gallon of water to a boil for 1 pound of Penne pasta. Add 1 tablespoon salt and boil pasta for 5 minutes. Drain. Put pasta into sauce. Sprinkle with Parmesan cheese.

Pesto (Basil Sauce)

The people of northern Italy, the Tuscans and the Genovese (from the Genoa region) are known all over the world for their Pasta Con Pesto, which is simply noodles with a pesto sauce. Pesto became the Pistou of France.

2 packed cups	fresh basil leaves, finely chopped
2 or 3 cloves	garlic, minced
½ cup	parsley, minced
½ cup	olive oil
to taste	salt and pepper
1 cup	Parmesan cheese, grated

Mix the basil leaves, garlic, and parsley in a bowl, add olive oil, a little salt and pepper, and as much as a cup of Parmesan cheese.

NOTE: It is always preferable to chop and mince pesto ingredients by hand; however, if you prefer you can put leaves with garlic, parsley, olive oil, salt, pepper and cheese into a food processor, but it will definitely taste different from that chopped on a board or crushed in a mortar.

VARIATIONS OF PESTO:

Pesto Coi Noci (Basil Sauce with Pine Nuts) is the same as the basic pesto, but pine nuts are added with the garlic and minced with the mixture.

Pesto Misto (Basil Sauce with Oregano or Marjoram) is made by using half basil and half oregano or marjoram in the mixture.

Pesto Acciugato (Basil Sauce with Anchovies) is made the same way but 2 or 3 chopped anchovies are ground with the basic basil mixture.

Basil sauce may be used on spaghetti, baked potatoes or Italian beans. It is also the secret ingredient which we add to minestrone soup.

A Tuscan meat market

Ravioli di Carne
(Ravioli with Meat Filling)

Various fillings for Ravioli (see Pasta Recipe)

½ cup	olive oil
2 pounds	pork roast, cut in cubes
to taste	salt and pepper
3 cloves	garlic, minced
1 large	onion, chopped
1 cup	water
2 stalks	celery, cut in 1 inch pieces
1 cup	combined fresh sage, rosemary, oregano, and parsley, chopped
3 pound	beef roast, cut in cubes
1½ pound	veal roast, cut in cubes
2 links	Italian sausage, removed from casing and crumbled
12	eggs, slightly beaten
1 cup	Parmesan cheese, grated
½ cup	bread crumbs
½ teaspoon	whole nutmeg, grated
¼ cup	sherry wine

Heat olive oil in a heavy saucepan. Brown pork with salt and pepper, garlic, onion, celery, combined herbs, and ½ cup of the water, adding more water as needed. Simmer until pork is tender. Remove pork from pan with slotted spoon and set aside. In same oil and drippings brown beef, veal, and Italian sausage. Remove from pan with slotted spoon. Grind all above meats and put in a large bowl. Combine with eggs, cheese, and bread crumbs. Blend thoroughly adding drippings from pan to make a moist, spreadable mixture.

NOTE: The above recipe makes about 50 dozen ravioli or 40 servings. When meat filling or other filling has been made continue by following recipe for Pasta con Uova (Egg Dough for Various Pastas, page 130) and freeze as instructed.

Ravioli di Formaggio (Ravioli with Cheese Filling)

1-14 ounce carton	ricotta cheese
½ cup	Parmesan cheese, grated
2	eggs, lightly beaten
½ cup	parsley, chopped
to taste	salt and pepper
½ teaspoon	nutmeg, grated

Mix all of the above ingredients.

Make ravioli according to Pasta con Uova (Egg Dough for Various Pastas).

Ravioli di Pollo (Ravioli with Chicken Filling)

¼ cup	olive oil
1 clove	garlic, minced
1 whole breast	chicken, boiled and chopped
1 cup	veal, ground
4 tablespoons	bread crumbs
2 tablespoons	Parmesan cheese, grated
2	eggs, lightly beaten
to taste	salt and pepper
1/4 teaspoon	nutmeg, grated

and, if you're real brave,

1	brain, boiled, drained, and finely chopped

Heat olive oil. Fry garlic until it begins to turn brown. Add chicken and veal. Fry 5 minutes and remove to a bowl. Add bread crumbs, cheese, eggs, salt and pepper, and nutmeg. And, if you're real brave, the finely chopped brain.

Make ravioli according to Pasta con Uova (Egg Dough for Various Pastas).

Ravioli di Spinaci (Ravioli with Spinach Filling)

2 pounds	spinach, cooked and chopped
1 whole breast	chicken, boiled and chopped
1 cup	bread crumbs
1 cup	Parmesan cheese, grated
4	eggs, lightly beaten
1 clove	garlic, minced
½ cup	parsley, chopped
to taste	salt and pepper
¼ cup	olive oil
1 cube	butter

Mix spinach and chicken with bread crumbs, cheese, eggs, garlic, parsley, salt and pepper. Fry mixture in olive oil and butter for about 10 minutes or until butter has been absorbed.

Make ravioli according to Pasta con Uova (Egg Dough for Various Pastas).

Salsa per Spaghetti (Spaghetti Sauce)

Weekends I usually make this sauce. On weekdays my son Frank Joseph usually passes by and raids the freezer taking containers of the sauce, bringing it home to his apartment for "spaghetti for my friends." Frank's closest friend, Paul Grisez, has produced a couple of movies to date. The friends are usually "traveling" together and I had the pleasure of their company on a recent trip to Los Angeles where we were royally entertained by Gary Lucchesi, another Tuscan boy from the Marina District, who found his niche by becoming a producer, thanked by Kevin Costner on television when he accepted his award for "Dances with Wolves."

½ cup	olive oil
½ cup	onion, chopped
1 clove	garlic, chopped
2 sprigs	fresh parsley, chopped
1 pound	sirloin, ground
1-28 ounce can	tomatoes, solid pack
1-8 ounce can	tomato sauce
1 cup	water
2 teaspoons	sugar
1 tablespoon	salt
1 teaspoon	dried oregano
6 leaves	fresh basil, minced
¼ teaspoon	pepper

In hot oil saute onion, garlic, parsley. Add ground sirloin and mix until well browned. Add tomatoes, tomato sauce, water, sugar, salt, oregano, basil and pepper and mix well. Bring to boiling, reduce heat and simmer covered and stir occasionally for 2 hours minimum. Cool and place in covered containers in freezer.

HELPFUL HINT: When bringing water to boil for pasta, dumplings, etc., always add 1 tablespoon of oil to water and a small handful of salt.

NOTE: Makes enough sauce for three times.

San Frediano

Salsa per Spaghetti del Cugino Dino (Spaghetti Sauce, Cousin Dino's)

My husband's cousin, Dino Ferrari, lives in Healdsburg, Ca. He has been married to Carol Davis from Oklahoma for 37 years. Carol's mother who lives in Windsor, Ca., a few miles from them, makes beautiful quilts which are truly an American art. Here is Dino's recipe for Spaghetti Sauce.

8 pounds	chuck beef, cut in cubes
4	yellow onions, diced
¾ head	celery, diced
2 cups	porcini mushrooms, dried, reconstituted and chopped
1 cup	fresh parsley, chopped
¼ cup	rosemary, removed from stalks and chopped
6 leaves	fresh sage, chopped
1-49½ ounce can	chicken broth, or
2½ pints	homemade chicken broth
3 cups	water
2-6 ounce cans	tomato paste
4-8 ounce cans	tomato sauce
8 cloves	garlic, finely chopped

Cut meat in 2 inch squares; put in large pot (no oil) over low heat and brown. Continue to cook until liquid has completely evaporated. Add onions, celery, mush-rooms, parsley, rosemary, and sage. Mix well and continue to cook over low heat about 10 minutes. Add chicken broth and water. Add tomato paste and sauce; bring to slow boil, reduce heat to a simmer and cook 6 hours, covered. Add garlic in the last 2 hours of cooking time.

NOTE: This recipe makes enough sauce for several times. Use 1 pint containers to store, then use 1 pint sauce for 1 pound of spaghetti, rigattoni, penne, or other store-bought, dried pasta.

Cousins Dino and Carol Ferrari

Salsa per Spaghetti Rustica (Spaghetti Sauce, Rustic Style)

½ cup	olive oil
2 cloves	garlic, finely chopped
⅓ cup	fresh parsley, chopped
6 leaves	fresh basil, chopped
7	tomatoes, peeled and chopped
to taste	salt and pepper
1 pound	spaghetti pasta
½ cup	Parmesan cheese, grated

In a frying pan put in olive oil to cover bottom of pan. Add garlic, parsley and basil and saute until limp. Add tomatoes, salt and pepper and cook for 5-8 minutes.

In 4 quarts of water cook spaghetti until tender to taste, drain, put in bowl, cover with sauce, mix well, and sprinkle with Parmesan cheese.

VARIATION OF RUSTIC SPAGHETTI: Salsa Di Vongole (Clam Sauce)

For a clam sauce, add 2-6½ ounce cans of clams and their juice as the last ingredient and gently heat.

Soffritto
(Basic Tomato Sauce)

A light sauce that can be used with any type of pasta, gnocchi, polenta or rice.

2	onions, finely chopped
½ cup	olive oil
4	tomatoes, peeled and chopped
to taste	salt

Gently saute onions in olive oil until limp but not brown. Add tomatoes, salt lightly and cook for 15 to 20 minutes until the mixture reduces to a thick sauce.

Ristorante "La Nina," Montecarlo, Lucca

Torre Guinigi

Spaghetti con Salsa di Funghi (Spaghetti with Mushroom Sauce)

1 pound	dried spaghettini or vermicelli
½ cup	olive oil
½ cup	dried porcini mushrooms, reconstituted
¼ inch slice	pancetta, chopped
½ cup	whipping cream
1-8 ounce can	tomato sauce
1 tablespoon	butter
3 tablespoons	Parmesan cheese, grated
to taste	pepper, freshly ground

Boil pasta 3 minutes and drain. Set aside in a serving bowl. Heat olive oil in small saucepan over medium high heat. Stir in mushrooms and pancetta. Reduce heat to medium and cook, stirring for 2 minutes. Add cream, tomato sauce, and butter, stirring well, until butter melts and sauce is warm. Pour sauce over pasta, top with Parmesan cheese and fresh ground pepper. Toss just to combine. Serve immediately.

Sugo di Carne
(Meat Sauce)

½ cup	olive oil
2	onions, chopped
2 tablespoons	parsley, chopped
¼ pound	pancetta, chopped
1	chicken breast, whole, skinned and deboned
3 links	Italian sausage, with meat removed from casings and crumbled
1 pound	pork, ground
to taste	salt and pepper
1 cup	red wine
¾ pound	fresh tomatoes, peeled
2 tablespoons	tomato paste
2 cups	beef broth
½ cup	Parmesan cheese, grated

Heat olive oil in saucepan over medium heat. Combine onions, parsley and pancetta. Add oil and saute until the ingredients are nicely colored, about 10 minutes.

Grind chicken breast coarsely in food processor. Add sausage, ground pork and chicken to the pan and season with salt and pepper.

Saute chicken and meats for about 15 minutes. Add wine and reduce for 10 minutes.

Puree tomatoes in food processor and add to pan along with tomato paste. Simmer for 20 minutes.

Add beef broth to the pan, cover and cook for about 1½ hours, using the remaining broth as needed so the sauce doesn't dry out.

Pour sauce over prepared pasta. Add cheese and serve.

HELPFUL HINT: If doorbell rings, add more wine to sauce.

CHI ABBIA BISOGNA, NON ABBIA VERGOGNA
He who is in need, should have no shame

Corn = Polenta

CONSIGLIO DI VECCHIO E AIUTO DI GIOVANE
Council of the old is the help of youth

Polenta and Rice

(Cornmeal and Rice)

Preparing Polenta for the festival at Pieve San Paolo

Gnocchi di Polenta (Coarsely Ground Cornmeal Dumplings with Prosciutto Sauce)

6 cups	water
2 tablespoons	salt
½ cube	butter
2 cups	polenta

PROSCIUTTO SAUCE

1 large, ½ inch slice	prosciutto, cut into chunks
1	onion, chopped
2	carrots, chopped
½ cube	butter
6 ounce can	tomato paste
to taste	salt and pepper
1 cup	water
½ cup	porcini mushrooms, reconstituted and chopped (optional)
½ cup	Parmesan cheese, grated

Heat water. Add salt and butter. When butter has melted and water is slowly boiling, pour polenta into water in a slow stream and, using a long wood spoon, stir constantly in order to avoid lumping. The cornmeal will thicken as it boils. Let boil very slowly for 40 minutes.

Meanwhile make the prosciutto sauce by sauteing prosciutto, onion, carrots, and butter. When vegetables are limp, add tomato paste, salt and pepper, and water and bring to a slow boil. Mushrooms can be added to recipe at this point. Let sauce simmer slowly about ½ hour.

When polenta is ready pour into a deep platter and let cool until it is set hard, about 1 hour. Invert polenta onto a chopping board and cut into 1 x 1 inch squares.

Into the deep sided platter lay out 1 layer of the 1 inch square Polenta. Sprinkle with Parmesan cheese. Add a layer of sauce (warmed up) and another layer of polenta, sprinkled with cheese and last layer of sauce.

If you are serving your guests cocktails, you can put this in a low oven until you are ready for dinner.

Prosciutto and Cheese

Polenta (Coarsely Ground Cornmeal Porridge)

While on campaigns the Roman soldiers were often fed PULS which was a wheat grain mixed with water to make a mush. It was either served warm or allowed to harden. Another version of this is POLENTA, a coarsely ground cornmeal, which appeared after corn was brought to Europe by Columbus. Polenta is available in Italian delicatessens.

1 cup	polenta
1 teaspoon	salt
4 cups	water
½ cube	butter
¼ cup	Parmesan cheese, freshly grated

Gradually add polenta (coarsely ground cornmeal) to boiling, salted water, stirring constantly until thickened. Cook in a heavy pan, stirring frequently, for approximately 45 minutes. Blend in butter. Serve as is with Parmesan cheese or with your favorite tomato, meat or vegetable sauce. Cold polenta may be sliced, brushed with butter and browned under the broiler.

Risotto (Braised Rice with Sausage)

Risotto is made with converted rice or with arborio rice. With converted rice the kernels separate; with arborio the dish is creamier.

3 tablespoons	butter
3 tablespoons	olive oil
3 links	Italian sausage, remove casings and crumbled
1 small clove	garlic, minced
1	onion, chopped
5 large slices	porcini mushrooms, reconstituted and chopped
1 cup	long grain rice or arborio rice
about 3½ cups	hot chicken or beef broth
to taste	salt
½ cup	Parmesan cheese, grated

Heat 2 tablespoons of butter and olive oil together in a dutch oven, add crumbled sausage and fry until brown. Add garlic, onion, and mushrooms and saute over medium heat until onions are golden. Add rice and stir until rice is well coated.

Add 1 cup of the broth, reduce heat, cover and simmer until most of the liquid has been absorbed, about 10 minutes. Add the remaining broth in 2 or 3 additions, removing cover each time and stirring lightly with a fork. Cook until the rice is tender and most of the liquid has been absorbed about 20 to 25 minutes longer. Exact amount of liquid needed and cooking time varies with rice and cooking pan you use. Taste, add salt if needed.

Remove from heat and add half the cheese and remaining 1 tablespoon butter, mix lightly with fork. Turn into a serving dish or serve from the casserole after topping with remaining cheese. Makes 4 to 6 servings as an accompaniment to meats or chicken.

A proud Tuscan

Risotto con Basilico
(Braised Rice with Basil)

1 tablespoon	butter
2 cups	olive oil
1 large	onion, chopped
2 cups	Arborio rice
¼ cup	dry white wine
7-8 cups, as needed	unsalted chicken broth
¼ cup	parsley, minced
6 leaves	basil, chopped
1 cup	Parmesan cheese, grated
to taste	salt

In a large saucepan melt butter with olive oil. Add onion and cook over low heat until the onion is soft. Add rice, stir until grains are well coated. Add wine, simmer, stirring until the wine is completely evaporated. Simmer slowly, stirring constantly adding chicken broth a ladle at a time. Continue stirring and adding broth. Mixture will gradually become creamy as the broth is absorbed by rice. After about ½ hour, add parsley and basil. Cook until rice is "al dente" and remove from heat. Add cheese and mix well. Season with salt.

Risotto con Fegati di Pollo (Braised Rice with Chicken Livers)

Serves 20

5	onions, chopped
½ cup	olive oil
3 pounds	long grain rice
4 quarts, as needed	chicken broth
to taste	salt and pepper
1 teaspoon	saffron
1½ cubes	butter
1½ pounds	mushrooms, sliced
1¼ pounds	chicken livers
½ cup	flour
1 cup	Parmesan cheese, grated

Cook 4 onions in oil until soft and yellow but do not let brown. Wash the rice and add it to the oil stirring constantly so that it does not stick. Add 3 quarts of broth, a little at a time, until the rice is tender but not soft, with each grain separated. Season with salt and pepper and add saffron which has been dissolved in a little extra broth.

Melt butter and brown mushrooms and the remaining onion in it. Add chicken livers, which have been rolled abundantly in the flour, and saute until brown. Add 1 quart of broth, season with salt and pepper and cook 15 minutes.

To serve: Put a spoonful of the risotto on very hot plates, make a slight depression in the top and put in a spoonful of the chicken liver mixture. Sprinkle with Parmesan cheese.

CHI VA A CACCIA SENZA CANI,
TORNA A CASA SENZA LEPRI
Who goes hunting without dogs,
comes home without rabbits

*The author's paternal cousins, Mario and Annie
Giovannini and Alma and Joseph Luchini*

Cousin Linda with her "right man," Richard Mann

Secondi

(Main Dishes)

A secret of Florentine cooking is the use of shallots instead of garlic.

A OGNI UCCELLO, IL SUO NIDO E BELLO
Every bird's nest is the most beautiful to him

Agnello alla Griglia (Barbecued Lamb)

Traditionally, we have a lamb dish on Palm Sundays. After the leg of lamb has been cooked, it is sliced thin and served on a very hot platter surrounded by small red potatoes (see page 270) which have been baked separately in the oven.

¾ cup	olive oil
½ cup	red wine vinegar
¼ cup	white wine
1-4 ounce can	green chiles, chopped
4 cloves	garlic, minced
1 teaspoon	each dried thyme, sage and rosemary
2 tablespoons	mustard, prepared
1-6 pound leg	lamb, deboned and butterflied
1-8 ounce can	tomato sauce
3 tablespoons	honey

Combine oil, vinegar, wine, chiles, garlic, herbs, and mustard. Mix well. Place lamb in a shallow dish and pour mixture over it. Turn to coat. Cover, refrigerate, and marinate overnight, turning once or twice.

Remove the meat from the marinade. Prepare the basting sauce by blending tomato sauce and honey into the marinade, stirring well.

Barbecue lamb over hot coals for 10 minutes on each side, basting frequently until done to your taste. Slice thin and serve with prepared mint sauce.

Every year, come October, my husband, Aldo, leaves.

He goes to Maxwell, Ca. where he and members of "The Club" go to shoot wild ducks. The Club is right next door to the Devlin Game Refuge, which is another word for a duck resort. The ducks eat there all day long and enjoy their "R&R." The ducks the members shoot are few and far between and I'm convinced that the ducks they do shoot are probably "thrown out" by their species.

There are stuffed ducks on my walls, on top of bookcases, paintings, etc., all over this house.

Members of the Club are: Billy Allen, Alberto Biancalana, Tyler Biggs, Vince De Martini, Aldo Figone, Mel Figoni, Willie Gherardi, Ron Langland, and Larry Lucchetti.

The ducks **that didn't get away** are sometimes cooked according to this recipe:

Anatra Selvatica (Wild Roasted Duck)

Alessandro Fillipini, Chef of Del Monicos called duck the "King of Birds."

5½ to 6 pound	wild duck
2 stalks	celery, cut in 3 inch pieces
1	onion, quartered
1	apple, quartered

Stuff duck with celery, onions and apples. Roast duck for about 1¾ hours in a 325 degree oven. Carve the duck and pass with the following sauce.

WILD DUCK SAUCE:

½ cup	red wine
3 to 4	peppercorns, crushed
1	bay leaf
pinch	thyme
1	shallot, chopped
½ cup	beef broth
1 tablespoon	brandy

Remove most of the fat from the roasting pan in which the duck was cooked. Add red wine to the pan, stir up all the brown juices and pour all of this into a small saucepan. Add next five ingredients. Simmer the sauce to reduce it by about half then add brandy and simmer briefly to evaporate the alcohol.

Arista di Maiale (Pork Roast)

½ cup	olive oil
2 cloves	garlic, smashed
2 stalks	celery, cut in pieces
4 small	carrots, cut in pieces
3 pound	loin of pork roast
1-8 ounce can	tomato sauce
½ cup	catsup
½ cup	red wine vinegar
½ cup	brown sugar
½ cup	dark corn syrup
½ cup	water
6 leaves	sage, chopped, or
1 teaspoon	dried Italian seasonings
1 tablespoon	cornstarch
4 tablespoons	sweet sherry

Put olive oil in a baking pan. Add garlic, celery, and carrots. Place pork roast on top of vegetables in a 350 degree oven for 2 hours. Combine next 8 ingredients. Cook over low heat in a pan for 5 minutes. Blend cornstarch with 2 tablespoons of the above mixture and return to pan, stirring until slightly thickened. Stir in sherry and cook for 10 to 15 minutes. Remove pan drippings from roast and add to this mixture. Cover meat with ⅓ of the sauce. Roast an additional 15 minutes and add another ⅓ of the sauce. Cook another 15 minutes. Remove from oven and place on a very hot platter with the remaining sauce. Total cooking time is 2½ hours.

Besciamella (Bechamel Sauce)

1 tablespoon	butter
1 tablespoon	flour
2 cups	whipping cream
to taste	salt and pepper
½ teaspoon	whole nutmeg, grated

Mix butter and flour stirring constantly for 2 to 3 minutes. Pour in cream, whisking to blend until smooth. Increase heat, whisking until sauce reaches full boil. Lower heat to simmer, season with salt and pepper. Simmer 10 minutes, stirring occasionally. Blend in nutmeg.

In 1988 the Archbishop of the San Francisco Catholic Archdiocese, John R. Quinn, appointed the Rev. John K. Ring to serve as pastor of St. Vincent De Paul. Every spring the men's club hosts a crab cioppino dinner. Since Father Ring is allergic to fish, they serve him a nice "bistecca."

Men's Club chefs.
Standing: George Moscone, Hank Cirby, John Johnck.
Seated: Chef in charge, Aldo Figone and Mario Alioto.
Missing: Raymond Pons.

*Rev. John K. Ring in front of Christmas altar decorated
by Joseph Figone.*

*Father Ring has completely remodeled the Altar at St.
Vincent De Paul and welcomes all to "come by and see" the
beautiful new interior of our church.*

Bistecca (Steak)

1	T-bone steak about 1½ to 1¾ inches thick
1 sprig	rosemary, dipped in olive oil (optional)
to taste	salt and pepper

Start the barbecue and wait until only hot ash remains, there should be no flame. Place the grill on barbeque so that it will get very hot. Grill should be about 3 inches from coals. When barbecue is ready, place steak on the grill with your hand, not with a fork, and cook for 5 minutes. Sprinkle with salt and pepper. Turn with spatula and cook 5 minutes on other side. Sprinkle again with salt and pepper and turn once more, cooking 5 minutes more on each side. This should be a medium cooked steak.

Serve immediately. If you like rosemary, dip a long sprig of rosemary in olive oil and brush steak periodically.

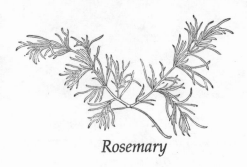

Rosemary

Cervello in Umido (Stewed Brains)

This dish is delicious, just don't tell them what it is and they'll love it!

2	calf's brains
1 tablespoon	parsley, chopped
½	lemon, juiced
1	carrot, chopped
1 stalk	celery, chopped
1 small	onion, chopped
to taste	salt and pepper
2 tablespoons	mayonnaise
2 tablespoons	milk

Wash brains in salt and water, removing membrane and leave in water for 30 minutes. Wrap brains in a piece of muslin and tie with a string. Put in a stew pan with water to cover and surround with chopped vegetables, seasonings, and lemon juice and cook for 20 minutes. Remove from the stew pan, untie, and serve on a hot dish with a mixture of equal parts of mayonnaise and milk.

Cervello Fritto
(Fried Brains)

2	calf's brains
3 cups	water
¼ teaspoon	salt
2	eggs, well beaten
½ cup	flour
to taste	salt and pepper
1	lemon, juiced

Wash brains in salt and water, removing membrane and leave in the solution for 20 minutes. Carefully remove and cut into ½ inch slices. Dip in a thick batter made with eggs, flour, salt, and pepper. Fry about 3 minutes on each side. Remove from pan with a spatula. Squeeze juice of a fresh lemon on each slice.

Coniglio Brasato (Braised Rabbit)

1-2 to 3 pound	rabbit
½ cup	olive oil
2 tablespoons	butter
2 cloves	garlic, smashed
3	carrots, sliced
6 leaves	sage, chopped
1 cup	white wine
4 cups	chicken broth
to taste	salt and pepper
about 1 cup	green olives (optional)

Have butcher cut rabbit in pieces.

In a medium size frying pan heat olive oil and butter. Add garlic. Brown rabbit on both sides. Add carrots, sage, and white wine. Continue to cook slowly until all wine is absorbed. Cover with chicken broth, add salt and pepper and let simmer about 1 hour or until rabbit meat can be pulled away from bone. If desired while cooking add a handful of green olives.

In 1964 our Pastor, Thomas O'Kane died and Archbishop McGucken appointed a new pastor to our parish church of St. Vincent De Paul in January, 1965. My husband, Aldo, became more active in our church because the new pastor was Monsignor William J. Clasby. My husband served in the Air Force at Geiger Air Force Base in Washington where he was in charge of the Officer's Mess. Monsignor Clasby retired from the Air Force as a bird colonel upon his appointment as our pastor. He was born in the parish and longed to return to it. It was a camaraderie between the two of them. Clasby would pick up the telephone and say "Hey, Figone, I have a visitor, a Commandant from the Air Force Academy, coming to town. What's for dinner tonight?" Many a time, we wound up with four or five Majors, Colonels, etc. coming for dinner. Monsignor's favorite dinner menu was spaghetti and breaded cutlets, vegetables and dessert. Clasby was a giant of a man, not only in stature but in his philosophies. Monsignor had been in charge of all the chaplains of the Pacific Theater during the 2nd World War and he never forgot it. He ruled St. Vincent De Paul with an iron hand and the parishoners and the students of the school loved it. Upon his retirement he took his entire Air Force pension and gave scholarships to the graduating students without anyone ever knowing who received them unless they said so themselves. Monsignor Clasby died in 1986 but his spirit is still felt in the attitude of his former pupils and parishoners.

Cotolettine Impanate (Breaded Veal or Beef Cutlets)

This recipe was originally for breaded veal cutlets but I find that it is much tastier if beef is used.

4	eggs, slightly beaten
to taste	salt and pepper
3 tablespoons	Parmesan cheese, grated
6 thin slabs	veal or top round, cut in 4 pieces each
1 cup	bread crumbs
½ cup	olive oil
2 cloves	garlic, smashed
2	lemons, quartered

Blend eggs with salt and pepper. Add Parmesan cheese and beat another minute. Dip meat in egg mixture and then in bread crumbs. Put olive oil in pan and add garlic. When oil is hot, remove garlic fry meat 1 minute on each side. Serve with quarters of lemon.

HELPFUL HINTS:
1. Always beat your eggs with a fork not a beater.
2. If meat is put in refrigerator for a minimum of an hour, bread crumbs will adhere better.

Fegato con Cipolle (Liver and Onions)

Every Saturday morning my father would arrive promptly at 9:00 a.m. to take my sons for a haircut, to play bocce ball, or to buy shoes. When he arrived, my beds had to be made and a full report given as to the day's activities. At noon the boys would go to his house and they would eat liver and onions (their favorite) with him. One Saturday I told him and my mother they couldn't come over for 3 or 4 days because we were painting the garage floor. Boy, was he mad! Instead we were decorating and setting tables and finally surprised him and my mother with a 35th anniversary celebration.

½ cube	butter
¼ cup	olive oil
4	red onions, thinly sliced
3 pounds	liver, thinly sliced
½ teaspoon	salt
¼ teaspoon	pepper
3 tablespoons	fresh parsley, minced
1-8 ounce glass	white wine
1	lemon, juiced

In a large skillet melt butter and oil over low heat. Add onions and cook stirring occasionally until very soft and light golden.

Take slices of liver, pat dry and add to the skillet. Increase heat to moderately high and saute stirring constantly until liver is browned outside, about 5 minutes. Add salt, pepper, parsley and white wine. Cook 5 minutes. Squeeze juice of lemon on top and serve at once.

Church in Pieve San Paolo

Fesa di Tacchino con Prosciutto e Formaggio (Turkey Breast with Italian Ham and Cheeses)

½ cube	butter
6 slices	turkey breast, ¼ inch thick
to taste	salt and pepper
6 thin slices	prosciutto
½ cup	chicken broth
½ cup	whipping cream
½ cup	mozzarella cheese, grated
¼ cup	Parmesan cheese, grated

Heat butter to foaming in a large skillet. Add turkey breast slices and cook 1 minute on each side, sprinkling each side with salt and pepper. Add slices of prosciutto to top of each turkey breast and chicken broth to pan. Continue cooking for 5 minutes. Set aside.

Combine whipping cream, mozzarella cheese, and Parmesan cheese. Spread over turkey and prosciutto slices and place under broiler until brown and bubbling.

Fesa di Tacchino (Sauteed Turkey Breast)

Turkey is a bird native to North America which was taken to Europe in the early 1500s. In Italy it soon became a substitute for the regal peacocks.

6 slices	turkey breast, ¼ inch thick
2 tablespoons	butter
to taste	salt and pepper
3	scallions, chopped
1 tablespoon	white wine
1 tablespoon	prepared mustard
1 dash	Worcestershire sauce
1 tablespoon	fresh parsley, chopped

Saute turkey breast slices in butter until lightly browned and cooked. Remove to heated platter and salt and pepper to taste. To pan juices, add scallions, white wine, prepared mustard, and Worcestershire sauce. Mix well and reheat slightly. Pour over turkey. Sprinkle with parsley and serve.

Fritto Misto
(Fried Meat Mix)

Make Besciamella Sauce and set aside. (See recipe, page 169.)

4	veal sweetbreads
4 sets	lamb brains
2	lemons, juiced
8 oz.	salami
1½ cups	besciamella sauce
as needed	flour, beaten egg and bread crumbs to coat meat
1	lemon, cut into wedges

Soak sweetbreads and brains in cold water for 1 hour. Drain and place into fresh water to cover and add lemon juice. Bring slowly to a boil. Boil ½ hour, remove from heat and drain. Skin sweetbreads. Preheat deep fryer to 375 degrees.

Now assemble:

Cut sweetbreads and brains into bite size pieces. Cut salami into ½ inch lengths. Dip salami into besciamella sauce and chill. Coat all ingredients with flour, eggs and bread crumbs in that order. Place ingredients into deep fry basket and allow to cook for 4 minutes. Turn onto a serving dish with a paper towel to drain and decorate with lemon wedges.

Involtini di Manzo
(Beef Birds)

2 pounds	bottom round of beef
¼ pound	prosciutto, chopped
4	anchovy fillets, mashed
3 tablespoons	Parmesan cheese, grated
4 tablespoons	dry bread crumbs
1	egg, beaten
3 tablespoons	butter
¼ cup	beef stock
½ cup	dry red wine

Slice bottom round into ¼ inch thick slices and pound each slice to a thickness of about ⅛ inch. Combine prosciutto, anchovy fillets, Parmesan cheese, bread crumbs, and egg. Mix well. Put an equal amount of the mixture on the center of each slice of beef. Roll up and tie with string. Brown beef rolls in butter over medium heat, turning often to brown all sides. Add beef stock and wine, cover and simmer 30 minutes. Remove to a warm serving platter and remove strings. Reduce sauce over high heat to thicken slightly. Pour over beef rolls and serve. Great with polenta.

Manzo con Piselli
(Top Round with Peas)

½ cup	olive oil
2 large	onions, finely chopped
2 cloves	garlic, finely chopped
1 teaspoon	dried thyme
1 teaspoon	lemon peel, grated
2	carrots, sliced in ¼ inch pieces
3 large	mushrooms, sliced in ¼ inch pieces
1-8 ounce can	tomato sauce
1	top round, first cut, 2 inches thick
1-10 ounce box	frozen peas
to taste	salt and pepper

In olive oil, fry onions, garlic, thyme, and grated lemon peel until onion is limp. Add carrots, mushrooms, and tomato sauce and cook until carrots are tender.

Add top round strips and cook 10 minutes. Add salt and pepper to taste. Add peas and cook an additional 5 minutes.

Serve with polenta or rice.

Osso Buco
(Veal Shanks)

4	veal shanks, cut in thirds
1 cup	flour
½ cup	olive oil
½ cube	butter
1 clove	garlic, smashed
½ cup	onion, chopped
½ cup	carrots, chopped
1 large	green bell pepper, seeded and cut in pieces
¼ cup	parsley, minced
2 tablespoons	tomato paste
2 cups	chicken broth
to taste	salt and pepper

Flour veal and brown slowly in olive oil and butter in a large casserole. Add garlic.

Remove meat from pan and carefully saute the next five ingredients, add 1 cup of chicken broth, then replace meat on top of vegetables and simmer over a very low heat for 1 hour. If sauce dries, add additional chicken broth but the shanks must cook the full hour. Salt and pepper to taste.

Pasticcio di Pasqua (Easter Pie)

4 links	mild Italian sausage
2 tablespoons	water
4	eggs, well beaten
15 ounces	ricotta cheese
4 ounces	prosciutto, chopped
2 ounces	salami, chopped
½ cup	mozzarella cheese, shredded
¼ cup	Parmesan cheese, grated
to taste	pepper
1 sheet	frozen puff pastry, thawed
4	hard-boiled eggs, sliced
4 thick slices	salami
¼ cup	parsley, minced

In a small skillet over medium heat, cook sausage links with water, covered, 5 to 6 minutes. Uncover and continue cooking, turning occasionally until lightly browned, about 12 minutes more. Set aside.

In a large bowl thoroughly blend ricotta cheese and beaten eggs. Slice 3½ links of sausage. Stir sausage, prosciutto, salami, and cheeses into ricotta mixture until well combined. Set aside.

On a lightly floured surface, roll puff pastry into 14 inch square. Cut 12 inch circle from the square. Line 9 inch pie plate with rolled pastry. (Turn pie plate upside down to cut out circle). Gather up what is left into a ball and roll out another circle. Make small slit with knife in circle. Cover this last circle with a larger plate while you continue.

Pour 1½ cups of the ricotta mixture into pastry lined plate. Keeping 1 center egg slice for garnish, arrange sliced eggs over ricotta mixture. Pour in remaining ricotta mixture. Sprinkle with pepper. Brush edge of bottom pastry with some beaten egg. Place slit circle on top of ricotta mixture. Seal edges of pastries together. Trim edge even with rim of plate. Flute edge of crust and brush top and edge with remaining beaten eggs. Bake in preheated 350 degree oven until lightly browned and knife inserted near center comes out clean, about 40 minutes. Garnish with reserved hard boiled egg slices, salami slices, ½ link sausage, crumbled and parsley. To serve cut into wedges.

MEGLIO UN UOVO OGGI CHE UNA GALLINA DOMANI
Better an egg today than a chicken tomorrow

Petti di Pollo
(Chicken Breasts)

3 whole	chicken breasts or 6 halves, deboned and skinned
to taste	salt and pepper
½ cup	flour
2	eggs, well beaten
1 cup	bread crumbs
2 tablespoons	olive oil
3 tablespoons	butter
1 teaspoon	each, dried sage, rosemary, and thyme
1	lemon, cut into quarters

Place chicken breasts between sheets of waxed paper and flatten by pounding with rolling pin. Sprinkle with salt and pepper. Dust lightly with flour, shake off excess. Dip pieces in egg then roll in bread crumbs. Press on crumbs with your palms to coat evenly. Shake off excess crumbs.

HELPFUL HINT: Coating will adhere to chicken better if placed in refrigerator for a couple of hours before frying.

Using 2 frying pans in order not to crowd chicken, heat oil and butter, but do not allow butter to brown. Put half the sage, rosemary, and thyme in each pan.

Add chicken, 3 or 4 pieces at a time. Cook over moderate heat until golden and crisp, tender inside but not dry, about 5 to 7 minutes on each side.

Drain on paper towels. Keep hot on warm serving platter until all is cooked. Serve with lemon quarters.

Piccioni Ripieni
(Stuffed Pigeons)

2	pigeons
1 small	onion, cut in half
1 piece	prosciutto, cut in chunks
to taste	salt and pepper
2 cloves	garlic, peeled
½ cup	red wine
6	sage leaves

Wash both plucked pigeons and drain well. Stuff the cavity of each pigeon with ½ onion, a small piece of prosciutto, salt and pepper, 1 garlic clove, and 3 sage leaves. Cook about ½ hour in 350 degree preheated oven in small loaf size pans. Pour the wine on top of each pigeon and continue cooking an additional ½ hour. Serve with risotto.

Pollo al Mattone
(Flat Chicken)

1-4 to 5 pound	fryer
½ cup	olive oil
2 tablespoons	butter
to taste	salt and pepper
1	whole nutmeg, grated
½	onion, chopped
1 clove	garlic, minced
½ cup	parsley, chopped
1 sprig	rosemary, stripped from stalks and chopped
6	potatoes, peeled and quartered

Have butcher split fryer down the back and butter-fly it, smashing it with the side of a cleaver. In a large frying pan heat olive oil and butter. Salt and pepper the fryer, lightly grate the nutmeg once or twice over the surface of the chicken. Place chicken in heated pan and put a large pie plate (to cover entire chicken) on it. Put a brick or a pot filled with water on top of the pie plate to put a heavy weight on the chicken. Fry slowly ½ hour until golden brown. In the meantime, prepare onion, garlic, parsley and rosemary. Chop all these ingredients until very fine. Turn chicken and sprinkle ingredients over fryer. Put weight back on and continue to fry another ½ hour until golden brown. Remove from pan and keep in a warm oven. In the meantime fry the potatoes in the same oil (add a little as needed during cooking). Cook potatoes until desired softness, turning frequently. Salt and pepper to taste. Remove fryer from oven, cut into pieces, put on platter and surround with potatoes.

A "Tuscan Delight" made by Joseph E. Figone in the San Joaquin Valley in California, a valley reminiscent of Tuscany.

Pollo con Prezzemolo (Chicken with Parsley)

4 pound	chicken, cut into serving pieces
to taste	salt and pepper
2 tablespoons	butter
½ cup	olive oil
1 clove	garlic, smashed
½ cup	dry white wine
¼ cup	chicken stock
1 tablespoon	fresh parsley, minced
½ small	lemon, juiced
2 tablespoons	butter

Season the chicken with salt and pepper. In a large frying pan, heat butter, oil, and garlic which has been smashed with the side of a knife. Brown the chicken on all sides over moderate heat for about 12 minutes. Cover the pan, reduce heat, and continue cooking the chicken for 10 minutes or until the meat is tender when pierced with a fork. Add dry white wine and simmer until it is reduced by half. Add chicken stock and simmer another 10 minutes. Arrange pieces of chicken on a hot platter and sprinkle with parsley. Add the lemon juice and reheat it, stirring well. Add butter and let it melt. Pour sauce over chicken and serve at once. It goes well with steamed potatoes or rice.

Red peppers

Pollo Saltimbocca
(Chicken, Rolled)

12	split chicken breasts (6 whole), deboned and skinned
12 thin slices	prosciutto
12 thin slices	Swiss cheese
2 cups	flour
2	eggs, slightly beaten
½ cup	bread crumbs
4 tablespoon	Parmesan cheese, grated
½ teaspoon	garlic salt
½ cube	butter
½ cup	chicken broth
½ cup	dry sherry
1 tablespoon	cornstarch
1 tablespoon	water

Pound the breasts with side of a mallet until ⅓ inch thick. Place a slice of prosciutto and a slice of cheese on top of chicken and roll. Skewer with toothpicks. Dip chicken rolls in flour to coat, then in beaten egg, drain briefly. Roll in a mixture of bread crumbs, Parmesan cheese, and garlic salt. Fry the rolls in butter in a large frying pan, turning to brown on all sides. Transfer to a baking dish. Pour on chicken broth and sherry. Bake uncovered in 350 degree oven for 30 minutes. Lift the chicken onto a serving platter and keep warm. Drain juices into a small saucepan, bring to a boil and blend in the paste of cornstarch and water, stirring constantly and cooking until thickened. Spoon sauce over chicken. Serve with rice, peas, salad and a dessert for a nice dinner.

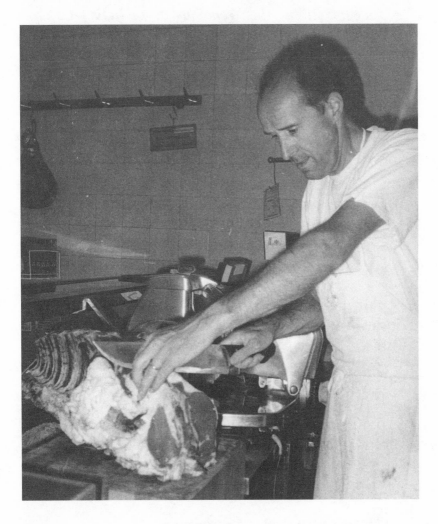

Butcher

Salsiccia
(Mild Sausages)

Mariano Barsotti, from my mother's home town of Pieve San Paolo, demonstrated this technique at an Italian Catholic Federation Heritage Day.

4 pound	pork shoulder butt, boned
¼ cup	salt
1 tablespoon	coarse black pepper
1 teaspoon	whole nutmeg, grated
1 teaspoon	allspice
1 tablespoon	fennel seeds, optional
2 cups	water
2 pounds	casings

Put boned pork shoulder butt through meat grinder (thick setting). Add salt, coarse black pepper, nutmeg, and allspice. If desired add fennel seeds. Mix with water, a little at a time, in order to keep mixture moist and pliable.

Take a small broom size cylinder and insert into casings or use the sausage making attachment of your food processor. Insert mixture into casings. Tie at desired lengths.

These sausages are freezable.

Salsiccia Dolce di Tacchino (Sweet Turkey Sausage Patties)

1 pound	turkey, coarsely ground
1 clove	garlic, crushed
1 teaspoon	fennel seeds (optional)
1 teaspoon	paprika
1 teaspoon	sugar
1 teaspoon	orange rind, grated
½ teaspoon	salt
½ teaspoon	black pepper, coarsely ground
½ cup	olive oil

Combine turkey in mixing bowl with next 7 ingredients. Mix thoroughly by hand. Shape sausage mixture into patties and freeze overnight on an ungreased cookie sheet. Next day, wrap frozen patties in heavy duty foil and seal tightly. Use within 4 to 6 weeks.

To cook, partially thaw frozen sausage cakes. (Sausage cakes cook better when partially frozen.) Preheat heavy skillet or saute pan 1 minute over medium heat. Put olive oil into pan and spread evenly. Add sausage cakes, reduce heat to low and cook, turning occasionally, for 5 minutes or until well browned on both sides.

Cheeses

Scaloppe di Tacchino con Formaggio Teleme (Turkey Cutlets with Teleme Cheese)

6-¼ inch slices	turkey breast
½ cup	flour
1 tablespoon	dried oregano, crumbled
2 tablespoons	butter
6 thin slices	Teleme cheese
¼ cup	Parmesan cheese, grated

Coat thin slices of turkey breast with flour seasoned with oregano. Saute in butter until lightly browned. Arrange slices on oven-proof platter and top with thin slices of Teleme cheese. Sprinkle liberally with Parmesan cheese and broil just until cheese melts and is bubbly.

Stufato di Pollo
(Chicken Stew)

1-3 pound	chicken plus gizzard, heart and liver
2 cloves	garlic, chopped
½	onion, chopped
½ teaspoon	allspice
½ teaspoon	nutmeg
½ teaspoon each	dried marjoram, oregano, basil, summer savory, thyme, rosemary, tarragon, sage
to taste	salt and pepper
1-28 ounce can	tomatoes, crushed
1 cup	dried porcini mushrooms, reconstituted and chopped (reserve broth)
½ cup	sour Italian green olives
3 stalks	celery, diced
3	carrots, diced
3	potatoes, peeled and diced
3 cups	chicken broth

Fry chicken and gizzard until well browned on all sides. Move ingredients to side and fry garlic and onions until limp. Add liver, heart, and seasonings. Fry until done. Add tomatoes and mushrooms with mushroom broth. Let simmer for 15 minutes. Add green olives, celery and carrots and cover pan with tight fitting lid. Simmer again for ½ hour. Add potatoes and continue to cook, adding chicken broth a little at a time, until potatoes and chicken are done.

Picking green olives by putting nets under trees and shaking trees.

Stufato di Agnello
(Lamb Stew)

---

2 pounds	lean lamb, cut into 1 inch cubes
½ cup	flour
1 teaspoon	ground black pepper
½ cup	olive oil
1	onion, finely chopped
½ pound	mushrooms, thinly sliced
½ cup	parsley, finely chopped
2 cloves	garlic, finely chopped
2	bay leaves
1 teaspoon	dried thyme
1 teaspoon	dried rosemary
2 cups	water
2 cups	dry red wine
2 small	potatoes, peeled and diced
2	turnips, peeled and diced
16 small	boiling onions
2 cups	shelled fresh peas

Put the cubed lamb, flour, and pepper in a paper bag and shake the bag until the meat is coated. Put olive oil in a large heavy frying pan. When meat is brown on all sides add onion and mushrooms and saute until onion is limp, remove mixture from pan and set aside. Do not wash the pan. Add parsley, garlic, bay leaves, thyme, rosemary, 1 cup of the water and 1 cup of the wine to pan. Simmer about 20 minutes. Return meat mixture to pan and add remaining cup of water and wine and simmer 30 minutes.

Add the potatoes, turnips, and boiling onions. Continue to simmer covered for 1 hour. About 10 minutes before serving, add the peas and cook until they are just tender. Serve with polenta.

Turnip

Tacchino Ripieno
(Turkey with Stuffing)

12 pound	turkey (retain neck, liver and gizzards)
1 teaspoon	salt
2 cloves	garlic, chopped
1 cup	fresh parsley, chopped
1 cube	butter
1¼ cup	olive oil
4 stalks	celery, chopped
½	yellow onion, chopped
½	red onion, chopped
4	eggs, beaten
to taste	salt and pepper
1 cup	Parmesan cheese, grated
1 teaspoon	poultry seasoning
½ teaspoon	nutmeg, grated
7½ ounce package	unseasoned bread cubes (used for stuffing)
retained	turkey broth

Remove neck, liver and gizzards from turkey. Wash and drain the turkey. Set aside.

Take the neck, liver and gizzards (with membrane removed) and boil in 2 quarts of water with 1 teaspoon of salt for about 45 minutes. Retain the broth. Remove meat from boiled neck and chop. Chop liver, heart and gizzards.

Melt butter with ½ cup olive oil in pan. Saute garlic and parsley slowly. Add celery, yellow onion, and red onion. Add chopped meats and mix well. Fry about 5 minutes.

Place this mixture in a large bowl; add eggs, salt and pepper to taste, unseasoned bread cubes, Parmesan cheese, and 1 cup of broth from turkey interiors to mix until slightly moistened. Add more broth as needed. Add poultry seasoning and nutmeg.

Place mixture by the spoonfuls into turkey and neck cavities. Truss using metal skewers, crisscrossing with heavy white string. Secure by knotting.

Rub outside of turkey with ¼ cup olive oil, sprinkle with additional salt, pepper and additional poultry seasoning. Pour ½ cup olive oil in roasting pan. Place turkey in pan and put in preheated oven, cooking at 325 degrees for 4 hours. (Peeled potatoes can be added1½ hours before end of cooking time.)

Tacchino e Zucchini
(Turkey and Zucchini)

6 thin slices	uncooked turkey, ¼ inch thick
¼ cup	Parmesan cheese, grated
½ cube	butter
2	zucchini, thinly sliced
½ cup	chicken broth
to taste	salt and pepper

Coat slices of turkey in Parmesan cheese and saute in hot foaming butter until very lightly browned. Remove to a warm platter.

To pan add zucchini, chicken broth, and salt and pepper. Saute zucchini until tender and arrange over turkey.

Timballo (Meat Pie) *Makes 2 pies*

Similar to Easter Pie (using chicken).

1 pound	sausage, casing removed and crumbled
1 pound	chicken, boneless, cut into ½ inch pieces
½ cup	onion, chopped
2 cloves	garlic, minced
½ cup	olive oil
1 cup	Parmesan cheese, grated
½ cup	mustard, prepared
3	eggs, slightly beaten
10 leaves	basil, minced
2	pastries for double crust 9 inch pies
5	basil leaves for garnish (optional)

In large skillet, over medium heat, brown sausage, chicken, onion, and garlic in olive oil. Remove from heat, drain well. Stir in Parmesan cheese, mustard, 2 eggs, and basil leaves. Roll half the pastry into an 11 inch circle. Place in 9 inch pie plate. Spoon filling into pastry lined plate. Roll remaining dough into an 11 inch circle, place over filling, trim, seal, and flute edges. Slit top of crust to vent. Cut pastry scraps into leaves to decorate top. Brush pie with remaining beaten egg. Bake at 375 degrees for 45 minutes before serving or until crust is brownish. Repeat for second pie. Garnish with the fresh basil leaf if desired.

Tonnato
(Veal with Fish Sauce)

1 leg	veal, boned
6 small	anchovies
1 small	onion, quartered
2	cloves
1	bay leaf
2 ribs	celery, chopped
½ cup	fresh parsley, chopped
to taste	salt

Remove the skin and fat from a leg of veal. Remove the bone and stick meat with 6 small fillets of anchovies. Tie and allow to boil for 1½ hours in a saucepan covered with water in which you have placed onion, cloves, bay leaf, celery, parsley and salt. Lift meat out of water (keeping broth for stock). Untie meat, cut in slices and place in a dish. Place in refrigerator and after a couple of days serve topped with sauce.

FISH SAUCE:

4 ounce can	tuna fish
2 additional	anchovies
¾ cup	olive oil
¼ cup	lemon juice
6	capers, chopped

Mince the contents of a can of tuna fish with anchovies and pass through a sieve adding olive oil and lemon juice. Add chopped capers.

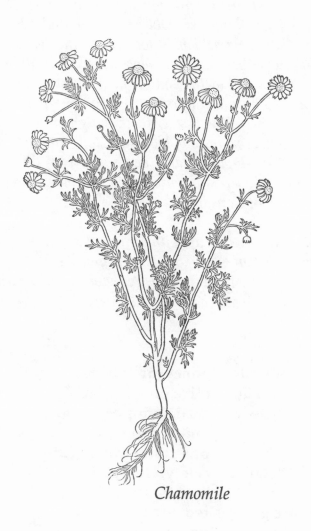

Chamomile

Trippa
(Tripe)

Each year for the Fourth of July my mother; her cousin, Maria Bomben; and her daughter, Dolores Maso; and I went to Calistoga, California which is located in the Napa Wine Region and stayed at a delightful place called Dr. Wilkinson's Hot Springs, located at the end of the main street, Lincoln Avenue. The family operators are Dr. John Wilkinson; his wife, Edy "Risso" Wilkinson; their daughter, Carolynne Wilkinson Clair; son-in-law, Howard Clair; grandchildren, Bettina and Christopher Clair, their son, Mark Wilkinson; and the Housekeeper-Supervisor with the most wonderful personality, Trini Gonsalez.

We have repeatedly met up with Margie and Johnny Green, Nancy and Stephen Kling and family, and Debbie and Eric Wertheimer and their son Jordon. We have our own barbecue and each year they ask that I cook the tripe.

2 pounds	honeycomb tripe
½ cup	olive oil
1 clove	garlic, chopped
1	onion, chopped
1 chunk	prosciutto, finely cut
2 stalks	celery, chopped
3	carrots, sliced
1-8 ounce glass	red wine
2	potatoes, cubed

1-28 ounce can	tomatoes, crushed
2 cups	water
2-16 ounce cans	red kidney beans, drained
½ cup	Parmesan cheese, grated

Purchase about 2 pounds of honeycomb tripe. Have the butcher cut it in ¼ inch strips. Boil the tripe for about 45 minutes.

In olive oil, fry garlic, onion, and prosciutto until onion is limp. Add celery, carrots, red wine and cook 5 minutes. Add tomatoes and simmer another 10 minutes. Add tripe and water.

Cover and cook 1½ hours over a low flame. While mixture cooks, add salt and pepper to taste. Add red kidney beans; however, if the front door bell rings at this point, don't drain the beans. Stir well and cook an additional 15 minutes. Remove from heat and serve with Parmesan cheese.

Vitella con Formaggio (Veal with Cheese)

4 thin slices	veal (leg cut)
¾ cup	olive oil
to taste	salt and pepper
4 thin slices	mozzarella cheese
3 cloves	garlic, finely chopped
1½ pounds	fresh tomatoes, peeled and chopped coarsely
1 tablespoon	dried oregano
1 tablespoon	parsley, chopped
2 teaspoons	Worcestershire sauce
1 cup	white wine
½ cup	Parmesan cheese, grated

Place olive oil into a heated pan, add veal, seasoned with salt and pepper. Lower heat and fry 1 minute on each side. Put slice of cheese on each veal slice, continue to cook 2 more minutes. Remove to heated platter reserving juices.

To juices add garlic, tomatoes, oregano, parsley, Worcestershire sauce and white wine. Cook slowly ½ hour.

Place veal and cheese in a baking pan, top with sauce, sprinkle heavily with Parmesan cheese. Some sauce can be reserved and passed separately at the table. Place under broiler until lightly brown. Serve.

HINT: Make sure that the mozzarella slices are very thin. Too thick and they thicken the whole dish. The veal slices take space in an average skillet. Repeating the whole process you can easily prepare 4 or more servings.

Although Worcestershire sauce is seldom used in Italian dishes it can be used in this recipe if you find it too bland. In Italy partially dried tomatoes are used in this dish; they have more flavor than our ripe tomatoes.

Bay

Vitella con Rognone (Breaded Veal Cutlets with Kidneys)

6	veal cutlets
4	eggs, well beaten
1 cup	bread crumbs
½ cup	olive oil
½ pound	mushrooms, sliced
1 sprig	rosemary, stripped from stalk and chopped
4 leaves	sage, minced
¾	onion, minced
½ cup	parsley, minced
1½ cups	tomatoes, solid pack

Bread veal cutlets with kidney by dipping in egg and then bread crumbs. Put in refrigerator several hours or overnight (crumbs adhere better).

Heat olive oil in a large frying pan. Fry on one side until golden brown and then turn and fry other side. Remove from pan. Drain oil through cloth or fine strainer until it is clear. In same oil saute mushrooms until tender. Add rosemary, sage, onion, parsley, and tomatoes. Simmer for 45 minutes.

NOTE: Many precut veal cutlets, bone in, come cut with kidney attached. Ask the butcher to cut if it is not in the meat case.

Vitella Arrosto (Veal Roast)

2 pounds	veal roast
1 tablespoon	butter
1 tablespoon	olive oil
1 small	onion, chopped
to taste	salt and pepper
4	bay leaves
2 teaspoons	thyme
1 clove	garlic, minced
½ cup	chicken broth, heated
2 large	carrots, cut in pieces
4 small	white onions

Buy a small veal roast weighing about 2 pounds. In a frying pan brown it slowly on all sides in butter and olive oil together with onion. Add salt, pepper, bay leaf, thyme, and garlic. Add ¼ cup chicken broth. Cover the pan tightly and let the veal cook over low heat for 45 minutes. Add carrots and white onions. Cook the veal for another hour turning from time to time and adding the remaining chicken broth as needed. The juices should be rich and brown and not too plentiful. Serve with plain boiled rice.

CHI VA PIANO VA SANO E LONTANO
Who goes slowly, goes safely and far

Desserts not being my forte, I am always looking for the "easy way out." One of my very favorites is Micro Fudge which is available in supermarkets and is produced by Richard Romano.

Micro Fudge is available in San Francisco's Marina Safeway which is not only the largest grocery in the area but also a gathering place for San Francisco Italians. How could it have missed with the following Italian contingent in its ranks: Store Director, Robert Iacopetti; Produce Department Manager, Lou Pignati; Meat Department Manager, Manny Machi; and Dairy Department Manager, Al Guaraglia.

"Ricky" Romano

Dolci

(Desserts)

Peter Joseph, Joseph Enrico, Frank Joseph

CHI NON SA FARE, NON SA COMANDARE
Who doesn't know had better not teach

Bigne di Crema di San Guiseppe (Saint Joseph Day Cream Puffs)

My father's name was Giuseppe (Joseph); every year we would celebrate St. Joseph's Day with family parties. Since I was an only child, we named our sons Peter Joseph, Joseph Enrico, and Frank Joseph. After Frank Joseph was born, my father hi-tailed it to the hospital and came into my room like gangbusters. The first thing he said to me in his broken English was, "Do me a favor, stop celebrating St. Joseph's Day." You see Peter was born on December 21 and Frank was born December 23. March 19 is St. Joseph's Day.

1 cube	butter
1 cup	water
1 cup	cake flour
4	eggs, unbeaten
1 tablespoon	sugar
¼ teaspoon	salt
1	lemon, grated peel

Put butter and water to boil in a saucepan. Add cake flour and stir until dough pulls away from sides of pan. Let cool. Add eggs, 1 at a time, mix well after each addition. Add sugar, salt and lemon peel. Divide dough into rounds the size of large walnuts. Place balls on baking sheet 3 inches apart. Put in preheated 400 degree oven for about 10 minutes, lower heat to 325 degrees and bake about 30 minutes or until golden brown. Cool, split and fill with zabaglione custard. (See page 262.)

Biscotti di Anice
(Anise Slices) *Makes 3 to 3½ dozen slices*

4 cups	flour, sifted
6 teaspoons	baking powder
2 cubes	butter
2 cups	sugar
2 teaspoons	anise extract
6 large	eggs
½ cup	sour cream
1 cup	almonds, blanched and thinly sliced, coarsely broken

Sift together flour and baking powder. Cream butter, sugar, and anise flavoring in a large mixing bowl. Add sour cream. Beat in eggs, one at a time. Add dry ingredients and almonds. Turn out on a floured pastry board and knead gently until smooth. Divide dough in half. Shape each half into a log shaped roll, ½ inch in diameter. Place on a lightly greased baking sheet. Bake in preheated 350 degree oven until firm to the touch, about 20 minutes. Remove from oven and let cool slightly. While still warm, cut rolls into slices about ½ inch thick. Place cut side down on cookie sheet. Return to 350 degree oven and bake until toasted, about 15 minutes. Turn once to toast and brown other side. Remove and let cool completely. Store in a tightly covered box.

HINT: Cut parchment paper to size of cookie sheets and/or baking pans and you will eliminate the need to grease and flour pans.

Almonds

Biscotti ai Pignoli
(Pine Nut Cookies)

1½ cups	sugar
1 tablespoon	almond paste
½ teaspoon	salt
4 large	eggs
3 cups	flour
½ teaspoon	baking powder
2 teaspoons	almond extract
2 tablespoons	pine nuts
2 tablespoons	powdered sugar

Preheat oven to 350 degrees. In a double boiler, bring water to a boil and, over boiling water, combine the sugar, almond paste, salt, and eggs. Beat mixture for 5 minutes. It should be lukewarm and resemble pancake batter. Almond paste should be well mixed in mixture. Remove from heat and continue beating another 5 minutes or until the batter is cool and looks like icing. Sift flour and baking powder together, fold gently into the batter. Fold in the almond extract using a teaspoon. Drop cookies 1½ inches apart on buttered and floured cookie sheets. Decorate with pine nuts and sprinkle with powdered sugar. Let stand 5 minutes. Bake for 15 minutes or until crisp on the outside.

Biscotti di Renata (Renata Baccei's School Cookies)
Makes about 80 large cookies

For the fifteen or so years when my sons Peter, Joseph, and Frank attended St. Vincent De Paul Grammar School at Green and Steiner Streets in San Francisco, the woman in charge of the cafeteria was Renata Baccei. The boys would always come home and rave about her cookies. Here is her recipe.

1½ pounds	unsalted butter
6 cups	brown sugar
6 cups	white sugar
8	eggs, separated
3 tablespoons	vanilla
4 teaspoons	baking powder
2-12 ounce packages approximately	chocolate chips
2½ pounds	flour

Melt butter, add sugars, mix thoroughly. Beat egg yolks and add to above. Add vanilla, baking powder, chocolate chips, and fold in beaten egg whites. Add enough flour to make a cookie consistency. Roll into a ball. Take small, walnut-size balls, space evenly on parchment paper covered cookie sheets and press flat with palm of your hand. Bake in 350 degree oven for 20 minutes.

Aerial View of Lucca

Budino
(Custard)

7	eggs
2 teaspoons	lemon juice
2 teaspoons	vanilla extract
1½ cups	sugar
4 cups	milk
½ teaspoon	whole nutmeg, ground
½ teaspoon	cinnamon
2 teaspoons	lemon rind, grated

Beat eggs together with lemon juice and vanilla extract. Add sugar, milk and stir. Place in a buttered baking dish, sprinkle top with nutmeg, cinnamon and grated lemon rind, then place in a larger baking dish filled with water. Place on lowest shelf of oven. Bake at 350 degrees for ½ hour or until knife inserted in center comes out clean.

VARIATION: If you like, take stale slices of panettone, cinnamon bread, leftover cookies, etc. and place on bottom of pan before pouring in liquid.

Cannoli
(Sweet Shells with
Egg Pudding with
Marsala)
Makes about 20

If you have never tasted cannoli, you're in for a treat. However, for the novice I recommend that you buy prepared cannoli shells in a bakery and then fill them yourself with the following recipe.

32 ounces	ricotta cheese
1½ cups	powdered sugar, unsifted
4 teaspoons	vanilla
½ cup	candied fruit, finely chopped
½ cup	candied orange peel
¼ cup	semi-sweet chocolate, chopped
1 cup	whipping cream (optional)

Mix ricotta cheese with a fork until very smooth. Blend in powdered sugar and vanilla. Add candied fruit, candied orange peel, and semi-sweet chocolate. Chill several hours or overnight and then fill tubes. For a fluffier filling fold 1 cup of stiff whipping cream into the above mixture.

NOTE: If you are brave enough to make the shells yourself, you can find tubes for cannoli in a houseware shop or you can buy lightweight aluminum tubing of one inch diameter and have it cut into 4 inch lengths.

TO MAKE SHELLS:

1¾ cups	flour
½ teaspoon	salt
2 tablespoons	sugar
1	egg, slightly beaten
2 tablespoons	sweet butter, cut in small pieces
¼ cup	sweet wine such as sherry, sauterne or madeira
1	egg white, slightly beaten
2 cups	shortening for deep frying
½ cup	powdered sugar

Sift flour with salt and sugar. Make a well in the center and place egg and butter in it. Stir with a fork, working from center out, moistening flour mixture a little at a time. While doing this add wine gradually, 1 tablespoon at a time, until dough begins to cling together. Use your hands to form dough into a ball. Cover and let stand for ½ hour.

Roll dough out on a floured board into a fairly thin sheet. Cut into 4 inch circles. With rolling pin, make a oval shape. Wrap around aluminum tubes. Seal edge with egg white. Turn out ends of dough from tube to flare. Fry 2 or 3 at a time in deep hot shortening for about 1 minute or until lightly golden. Remove with tongs to paper towels to drain. Let cool about 5 seconds then slip out tube holding on to shell carefully. Cool shells completely before filling.

The easiest way to fill is to use a pastry tube or small teaspoon. After all shells have been filled, sprinkle with powdered sugar.

Castagnaccio
(Chestnut Pancakes)

Chestnuts have often been the principal food of the poor. After the collapse of the Roman Empire, many Italians were reduced to a diet of chestnuts eaten boiled or roasted. On Corsica, where the Franceschis were originally from and would return to from time to time, chestnuts were used in place of potatoes. A cheap substitute for bread, they are often referred to as the Corsican bread. On Corsica chestnuts are kept in drawers, hence when families eat cheaply on Corsica they are said to "Eat out of the drawer."

Chestnut flour is available in packages in specialty stores. Chestnuts are picked in October and November and milled in November, so the freshest flour arrives in the United States about December of each year.

2½ cups approximately	chestnut flour
1 cup	olive oil
¼ teaspoon	salt
4 teaspoons	sugar
1½ cups	cold water
½ cup	pine nuts
½ cup	raisins, soaked for ½ hour
1 sprig	rosemary
¼ cup	orange peel, grated
4 ounces	walnut halves
8 ounces	ricotta cheese

Put chestnut flour in a bowl. Add 5 tablespoons of olive oil, a pinch of salt, and sugar. Slowly add cold water until the consistency of a pancake batter. Add pine nuts and drained raisins. Mix all ingredients well. Put ½ cup olive oil in a heavy skillet. Pour batter in skillet (oil will come up sides). Remove leaves from a sprig of rosemary and spread evenly over entire surface of pancake. Grate orange peel over surface. Place walnut halves on top of batter. Spread another tablespoon of olive oil over surface of pancake by drops. Put in a 350 degree preheated oven for 45 minutes. Remove from oven. Serve with a scoop of ricotta cheese on the side or spread on top of pancake.

Land of the Chestnut Trees

Cialde
(Rolled Cones)

6	eggs, well beaten
1 cup	butter, melted
1 teaspoon	each, lemon and anisette extract
3½ cups	flour
1½ cups	superfine sugar
4 teaspoons	baking powder
1 quart	ice cream

Beat eggs and add sugar gradually, beating until smooth; add cooled melted butter. Add extracts. Sift flour and baking powder together; add to egg mixture. Dough will be smooth enough to drop by teaspoons.

Drop a teaspoonful in Cialde grill (aka pizzelle grill). Cook about 30 seconds or until nice and brown, do not turn. Remove from Cialde grill and quickly roll, browned side out. Set aside to cool. Serve with favorite ice cream.

Crema Fritta (Fried Cream)

2½ cups	milk
½ cup	sugar
1	lemon rind, grated
⅓ cup	regular cream of wheat or semolina flour
¼ teaspoon	vanilla
1	egg, beaten
1-9 ounce package	plain bread crumbs
2 tablespoons	butter
2 tablespoons	oil

Bring milk, sugar, and grated lemon rind to a boil. Slowly sprinkle in cream of wheat or semolina, stirring constantly while it thickens. Lower heat, cook for 10 minutes. Remove from heat, add vanilla, and stir.

Pour mixture into a flat dish with sides. Allow mixture to cool. Cut into squares and dip in beaten egg then in bread crumbs and fry in butter and oil. Brown on both sides and serve hot.

Lucca

Croccante
(Peanut Brittle Cake)

---

1 tablespoon	unflavored gelatin
½ cup	cream sherry
1¾ ounce package	vanilla pudding mix
1½ cup	milk
¼ cup	honey
1 cup	whipping cream, whipped stiff
1-9 inch	pie shell
1 cup	peanut brittle, coarsely crushed

Soften gelatin in sherry. Prepare pudding mix according to package directions using milk as liquid. Remove cooked filling from heat, add softened gelatin, and stir until dissolved. Stir in honey. Cool filling completely, about 1 hour, and when partially thickened, fold in whipping cream. Spoon into pie shell.

Cover top with crushed peanut brittle patting it down with the palm of your hand. This croccante cuts into perfect wedges if it has been chilled overnight. If you like you can substitute pine nuts or coarsely chopped walnuts for the peanut brittle.

Crostata di Prugne (Palazzo Prune Tart)

About 10 servings

approximately

2 cups	prunes, pitted
8 ounces	apricot halves, dried
½ cup	cream sherry
¼ cup	frozen orange juice concentrate
½ cup	water
1¼ cups	graham cracker crumbs
¾ cups	fresh bread crumbs
3 tablespoons	vegetable oil
3 tablespoons	honey
1-10 ounce jar	sweet orange marmalade, melted

In a saucepan combine prunes, apricots, sherry, orange juice concentrate, and water. Bring to a boil, reduce heat, and simmer 15 minutes. Cover, let stand until completely cool and most of the liquid has been absorbed.

In a mixing bowl, combine graham cracker and bread crumbs, oil, and honey. Mix thoroughly to blend. Press evenly into bottom and sides of a 9 inch tart pan with removable bottom. Bake in 400 degree oven 10 minutes. Cool. Brush bottom of shell with about 1¼ cups of the marmalade. Arrange prunes and apricots decoratively in shell. Stir any remaining juices from fruit, about 1 or 2 tablespoons, into the remaining marmalade. Spoon evenly over fruits in tart shell. Chill thoroughly before cutting into wedges and serving.

Frittelle di Castagne (Chestnut Fritters)

1 cup	chestnut flour
as needed	water
pinch	salt
¼ cup	seedless raisins
⅓ cup	pistacchio nuts, chopped
2 cups	olive oil for deep frying
½ cup	powdered sugar

To chestnut flour, add enough water to make a thick paste. Add salt, seedless raisins, and pistacchio nuts. Mix well and drop by spoonfuls into deep hot oil, cooking until golden brown. Drain, sprinkle with powdered sugar.

Macedonia
(Fruit Cup)

¼ cup	seedless raisins
¼ cup	dry white wine
½ cup	fresh and/or dried fruits such as melons, strawberries, cherries, raspberries,, nectarines, or peaches
1	apple
1	orange
1	pear
small bunch	red grapes
3 or 4	pitted dates
3 or 4	figs
½	lemon, juiced
2 heaping tablespoons	superfine sugar
1 jigger	maraschino liqueur
1	banana

Put raisins to soak in wine. Chop apple, orange, and pear into bits and put into a big bowl. Slice grapes in half, discarding any seeds, and add to other cut fruits. Chop dates and figs and add to above. Pour in the raisins and wine. Add juice of half a lemon, sugar, and maraschino liqueur. Stir gently with a big spoon to get juices running. Chill for ½ hour. Before serving add sliced banana and stir gently once more and serve.

Maddalena (Sponge Cake)

5	eggs, room temperature
1 cup	sugar
½ cup	unsalted butter, melted
1 cup	flour

Heat oven to 400 degrees. Lightly butter a shallow 10 inch cake pan. Sprinkle with flour, tapping out excess.

Beat eggs in a large bowl at high speed until foamy. Gradually beat in sugar, 2 tablespoons at a time, and continue to beat until mixture is pale and tripled in volume; this will take about 10 minutes.

Remove 1½ cups of beaten egg mixture to another bowl. Drizzle melted butter over mixture, gently fold in with spatula. Gently fold butter-egg mixture back into egg mixture in first bowl. Sift flour in 3 batches over mixture while gently folding in with spatula. Fold just until all the flour is incorporated.

Gently pour batter into prepared cake pan using a spiral motion working from outside edge of pan toward center. Bake on center rack of oven until top of cake springs back when lightly pressed, about 40 minutes. Cool cake on wire rack. Remove from pan and continue cooling on rack to room temperature. Immediately wrap cake in plastic wrap and allow to remain at room temperature for 2 days before serving.

A beautiful garden in back of an Italian home in Northern Italy (the home of Restauranteur Modesto Lanzone).

Pane di Noce e Zucchini (Zucchini Nut Bread)

Makes 2 loaves

3	eggs
1 cup	vegetable oil
2 cups	sugar
2 cups	zucchini, peeled and grated,
2 teaspoons	vanilla
3 cups	flour
1 teaspoon	baking powder
1 teaspoon	salt
3 teaspoons	cinnamon
½ to 1 cup	walnuts, chopped

Beat eggs until light and foamy. Add next 4 ingredients. Mix lightly but well. Sift remaining ingredients except nuts in separate bowl. Add flour mixture to first mixture and blend. Fold in nuts. Put in greased 9 inch loaf pans. Bake at 325 degrees in a preheated oven for 1 hour.

SIENA is the home of the annual Palio, a horserace around the main square in which all the riders dress in medieval costumes. The race, which is held each August, lends a festive air to the whole town. Banners hang from each balcony. The city, built around the square in a circle fashion, consists of the quarters known as the Banchi Di Sopra and the Banchi Di Sotto. The cathedral is a masterpiece of black and white marble. Siena is one of the few towns in all of Italy in which automobiles are not permitted and so one must walk. This rule has existed for many, many years and has recently been applied to more and more cities of Italy including Lucca.

Siena is the home of St. Catherine of Siena, a Doctor of the Catholic Church. St. Catherine never became a nun but lived at home as a member of the Third Order of the Dominicans. Her house, which exists in its original condition, is entered by way of a garden. The garden and the kitchen are on one level. The other rooms continue down the hill to the lower street level.

Monte Dei Paschi Di Siena, founded in 1472, is the largest bank with branches throughout Italy.

When a child is born in Siena, a kerchief is placed around his neck with the colors of his District or Contrada, and throughout his life the colors accompany him. When an Italian arrives in Siena and registers at a Hotel, if his Italian name is a Sienese name, it is immediately recognized and the colors of his contrada (district) are hung from the flagpole of the hotel. The contrade are: Aquila (eagle), Chiocciola (snail), Capitana dell'onda (flagship of the wave), Pantera (panther), Selva (forest), Tartaruga (tortoise), Civetta (owl), Leocorno (horned lion), Nicchio (conch), Valdimontone (vale of the ram), Torre (tower), Bruco (catepillar), Drago (dragon), Giraffa (giraffe), Porcospino (procupine), Lupa (she-wolf), and Oca (goose). Of these, ten are drawn by lot to take part in the Palio twice a year on July 2 and August 16.

Siena is a tranquil city with none of the bustle found in other cities of Italy. It is a safe city where one can travel night and day without fear. The language of Siena is the "mother tongue" of Italy and is taught in schools throughout Italy as it is considered to be the "purest of tongues."

The restaurants are outstanding and few have ever changed ownership. Proprietorship is passed from father to son or daughter for the women of Siena have the same status as the men and have enjoyed these privileges since Medieval times.

A few of my favorite restaurants are: Alla Speranza, Al Mangia, Altri Tempi, Antiporto, Beppino-Le Campane, Biagi, Carnesecchi, Da Dino, Due Pini, Grotta S. Caterina, Il Biondo, Il Campo, La Diana, La Pace, Lo Stellino, Minerva, Nuove Donzelle, Rustichetto, San Giovanni, Sotto Le Fonti Da Rocco and Turiddu.

Restaurants throughout Tuscany are all excellent but there is something about the way Sienese greet their customers that tends to add graciousness to an already gracious city.

Panforte di Siena
(Fruitcake of Siena)

The wafers that are consecrated and used during Catholic Church communion services, are made in large rounds and are placed on the bottom of panforte rounds when they are removed from the oven.

1 cup	sugar
½ cup	water
3 tablespoons	honey
1 pound	candied fruit
1 cup	flour
1 teaspoon	coriander, ground
1 teaspoon	cloves, ground
1 teaspoon	mace, ground
1 teaspoon	whole nutmeg, grated
1 teaspoon	cinnamon, ground
1 teaspoon	cocoa powder
1	orange, grated peel
1	lemon, grated peel
1 cup	almonds, toasted, chopped and peeled
1 cup	hazelnuts, chopped

Melt sugar with water. Bring to a boil until syrup drips from spoon in a steady stream. Remove from fire. Add candied fruit and next 7 ingredients, sifted. Return to stove and let boil slowly for 10 minutes. Add orange and lemon peels and chopped nuts until a thick paste is formed. Butter and flour an 8-inch spring form cake pan. Flour your hands and pat down mixture. Bake in 325 degree oven for 1 hour. Cool slightly then remove sides of pan. Sprinkle top with confectioners sugar.

Sciroppo
(Rum Sauce)

1½ cups water
1¼ cups sugar
½ cup dark rum
2 tablespoons vanilla

Combine water and sugar in heavy saucepan. Heat over medium heat, stirring occasionally to simmering. Cover and simmer 5 minutes. Remove from heat, let cool slightly, and stir in rum and vanilla. Cool to room temperature. Refrigerate covered. Can be stored covered in refrigerator for up to 6 months. Makes about 2 cups. Good served with ice cream.

Torta di Crema
(Cream Cake)

1 cube	butter
½ cup	vegetable oil
2 cups	sugar
5	eggs yolks, reserve egg whites

Beat together until creamy, then add the following ingredients:

1 cup	buttermilk
1 teaspoon	soda
2 cups	flour
1 cup	flake coconut

Beat the reserved egg whites and fold into the above mixture. Pour into three 8-inch layer cake pans and bake at 350 degrees for 30 minutes.

ICING:

8-ounce package	cream cheese
½ cube	butter
1 pound	powdered sugar
1 teaspoon	vanilla
1 cup	favorite nuts, chopped

　　　　1 can　　crushed pineapple, drained
　　　　1 jigger　amaretto liqueur

Combine and spread between layers and on top of cake when cake is completely cool.

Torta di Ricotta con le Mandorle (Ricotta Cheesecake with Almonds)

Serves 16

This cheesecake is creamy in texture and the almonds offer a crunchy surprise. Enjoy!

CRUST:

1¼ cups	graham cracker crumbs
6 tablespoons	butter, melted
¼ cup	sugar
¼ cup	almonds, finely chopped

Preheat oven to 350 degrees; combine crumbs, melted butter, sugar, and almonds. Blend thoroughly and press mixture on bottom and partly up sides of a 9 inch spring form pan. Bake for 10 minutes. Chill before filling.

FILLING:

32 ounces	ricotta cheese
½ cup	sugar
4 large	eggs
1 tablespoon	corn starch
1 teaspoon	almond extract

1 cup   whipping cream
½ cup   almonds, finely chopped

Drain the ricotta of any liquid. In a large mixing bowl or food processor combine ricotta cheese and sugar and beat thoroughly. Add eggs, corn starch, almond extract, cream, and almonds, beating thoroughly again. Pour mixture into cooled pan and bake at 350 degrees for 1 hour or until a cake tester comes out clean. Prop the oven door open and allow cake to cool for an hour. Then remove from oven and cool to room temperature. Chill thoroughly.

Editor, Judy Kimball, whose Almond Ricotta Cheesecake appears above, and the author.

Torta al Rum
(Rum Cake)

CAKE:

1½ cups	flour
1½ teaspoons	baking powder
3	eggs
1½ cups	sugar
¾ cup	milk
3 tablespoons	butter

FILLING:

½ cup	light rum
½ cup	almond liqueur
2 cups	whipping cream
1 tablespoon	powdered sugar
¼ teaspoon	vanilla
1 square	semisweet chocolate, grated
4 ounces	ricotta cheese
¼ teaspoon	cinnamon, ground
¼ teaspoon	whole nutmeg, grated
¼ cup	blanched almonds, chopped

Grease a 9 inch spring form pan. Combine flour and baking powder. In a small mixer bowl, beat eggs at high speed 4 minutes or until thick. Gradually add sugar, beat at medium speed 5 minutes or until light.

Add flour mixture to egg mixture and beat at medium speed until just combined. Heat milk with butter until butter melts then add to batter, beating until combined. Turn into prepared pan. Bake in 350 degree oven about 50 minutes or until toothpick comes out clean. Cool on rack about 30 minutes. Remove from pan. Cool completely.

Cut the cake horizontally into 3 layers. Mix together rum and almond liqueur. In a large bowl, combine whipping cream, powdered sugar, and vanilla. Beat until soft peaks form. Place 1 layer on serving plate and spoon ⅓ of rum mixture over cake. Top with ¼ of the whipped cream mixture. Sprinkle with some chocolate. Repeat. Top with last layer. Make holes in top layer with a fork and pour remaining rum mixture over surface.

Take remaining whipped cream and add ricotta, cinnamon and nutmeg. Spread over top and sides of cake. Sprinkle remaining chocolate over top. Press almonds around sides of cake. Chill overnight.

Torta di Cioccolata e Mandorle (Isle of Elba Chocolate Almond Torte)

1 cup	unsalted butter, softened
2 cups plus 2 tablespoons	confectioner's sugar
2 ounces	semi-sweet chocolate, cut into quarters
8 ounces	almonds, ground (about 1¾ cups)
5	eggs, separated
1 package	dry yeast
	vanilla ice cream (optional)

In a large mixing bowl, beat butter with sugar until creamy. Put chocolate in bowl of food processor. Process until finely grated, consistency should be like cornmeal. Add half of this ground chocolate, half of the ground almonds and 2 egg yolks to butter and sugar. Mix until well blended. Add remaining chocolate, almonds and 3 egg yolks to batter and mix to blend.

In a clean bowl, beat egg whites until fluffy. Pour whites onto batter. Sprinkle yeast over whites then gently fold whites into batter. This will be difficult at first because batter is stiff but after a few strokes, it will be mixable.

Pour batter into a parchment-covered 9-inch spring form pan. Bake at 375 degrees about 40 minutes or until top springs back when touched lightly. Cool in pan or on wire rack. Run knife around pan to loosen, then remove the ring. Transfer cake to a serving platter after removing from base. Sprinkle with confectioners' sugar and serve with vanilla ice cream. Cake is best served warm or at room temperature.

Corsagna church and chapel where my cousin, Mon-
signore Don Sergio Giorgi, has been pastor for sixty years.
This year my son Joseph Enrico stayed with Don Sergio for
3 months.

Monsignore Don Sergio Giorgi and Pope John Paul.

Corsagna

My paternal grandmother's name was Carmelinda Giorgi (Giovannini). Her brother, Cavaliere Marco Giorgi, had a son, Sergio Giorgi, who became the pastor of Corsagna (above Bagni Di Lucca), north of Lucca. Monsignore Giorgi lives on the very top of the mountain and the town surrounds the church and rectory.

Corsagna may not be the end of the earth but, believe me, you can see it from there.

A few years ago my mother and I stayed there for a week. At the end of the week it was getting on my nerves—up the hill, down the hill, up the hill, down the hill, not to mention the perpetual power shortage in Italy, but that's to be expected, the whole town was on one power line.

At any rate, Saturday, I started packing and Don (Rev.) Sergio got panicky. "I've got all the neighboring bishops and priests coming to dinner Sunday. Who's going to cook?" That has been a standard question in my house! Who's going to cook? Well, we stayed another week and this is the menu we had (naturally Italian American)!

Plates of antipasto consisting of thin slices of melon and prosciutto (page 51) surrounded by slices of salami, mortadella, etc.

Chicken Broth (Brodo di Gallina) with pastina (page 94)
Boiled beef and boiled chicken, drained from above
    recipe (page 94)
Roast veal (Vitella arrosto) surrounded with Italian
    green beans (page 215)
Torta garfagnana (page 256)

Naturally they were all agape. An American (Italian) had beat them at their own game, the cooking and eating game.

Torta Garfagnana (Cake of the Garfagnana Region)

This cake is made in the Garfagnana region of Tuscany and is served last after a big meal. Even though I am not the world's greatest baker, I realize that this is a very temperamental cake. The Garfagnana region is at the bottom of the Italian Apennines and the weather there is always mild. If I try baking this on a warm day it is usually a failure. Baked on a 50 to 60 F temperature day, it's perfect.

1½ cup	almonds
2½ cups	sugar
3 cubes	butter, melted and cooled
5½ cups	sifted flour
2 tablespoons	anise seed
1	lemon, grated peel
6	eggs
2 shot glasses	cherry brandy
1⅓ cups	milk
2 tablespoons	cream of tartar
2 teaspoons	baking soda

Drop almonds into boiling water with 2 teaspoons of sugar for 2 minutes. Drain, peel, dry with a cloth, then chop fine, or use a package that equals 1 cup of chopped almonds.

Use about 2 teaspoons of the butter to grease a large pan (preferably with spring sides) then flour pan lightly. In this case do not cover pan with parchment paper. Melt the remaining butter over a very low flame. Allow to cool. Preheat oven to 375 degrees.

Put sifted flour, sugar, almonds, anise seed, and lemon rind in a large bowl, mix well. Make a hole in the center of this dry mixture, break eggs into it, add butter, and cherry brandy. Work everything together until mixture is smooth. Mixture will be heavy and not pourable.

Warm the milk in a very large pan, add cream of tartar, and baking soda. It will then foam up. When it foams, add to heavy mixture and stir in order to blend well. Pour into prepared cake pan, put into preheated oven and bake for about 1 hour at 375 degrees (note higher temperature) or until a toothpick stuck into the center comes out dry. The top of the cake will be cracked in several places. This is characteristic. Remove from oven and serve warm with Zabaglione Sauce or cold.

NOTE: This cake is flavored with anise seeds. The Romans ended their banquets with anise flavored cakes which they claimed aided the digestion.

Torta Toscana (Fruitcake from Tuscany)

Makes 4 pies

1 cup	parsley, chopped
3 bunches	Swiss chard, boiled, chopped, and drained
1 cube	butter
2 shot glasses	rum
2 shot glasses	sherry or other sweet wine
1 loaf	stale French bread, soaked in water, drained and crumbled
1 teaspoon	cinnamon, ground
1 teaspoon	nutmeg, ground
1 teaspoon	allspice, ground
½ teaspoon	dried thyme
2 cups	sugar
½ cup	pine nuts
½-15 ounce box	golden raisins, soaked and drained
2 teaspoons	vanilla extract
2 cups	Parmesan cheese, grated
2 teaspoons	lemon extract
6	eggs, slightly beaten
4	pie shells

Saute Swiss chard and parsley in butter. Cool. Mix all ingredients together, place in pie shells and cook for 45 minutes or until pie crust is golden brown.

We have been baking Torta Toscana in the family for generations but the best dough for the Torta I discovered thirty-four years ago when Edith Del Prete and her husband Amerigo moved next door to us. San Francisco houses are connected and through the lightwells, you can see into your neighbor's kitchen and vice versa. When Edith and Amerigo and their children Gino, Norma, and Aldo moved in, we had a bar across the landing of the back stairs, but I was pregnant with my first born son, Peter, and in order to facilitate my going back and forth, we removed the bar and we could just walk into each other's back doors. The years have passed by quickly and Amerigo and Edith retired as owners and operators of Panama Canal Ravioli on Grant Avenue. Their son Gino became famous with the opening of The Condor, the first topless nightclub in San Francisco. He has a daughter, Gina, who was born the same day as my son, Joseph. Edith and Amerigo's daughter, Norma "Cookie," married James Hadnot, Sr. of the Sacramento Kings basketall team (one of the first interracial marriages in the Italian community, a marriage that has lasted over 30 years) and they had two lovely children, the beautiful Julie who now works in Washington D.C. for Congressman Ronald V. Dellums, and James, Jr. "JJ" who died recently at 21 years of age. Edith and Amerigo's son Aldo, with the same name as my husband, was married to an Irish girl, Pat McGrath, and they had two children, Analisa and Ricky. Aldo died this year (1991). Ricky is our godson. All these people have always referred to me as "Sai" because when the godson Ricky was small, he couldn't say Aunt (Zia) in Italian and it would always come out as "Sai" and so I was stuck with the nickname.

This then is the recipe for Edith's pie dough which I use for the Torta Toscana.

PIE CRUST FOR 4 TORTES:

4 cups	flour
1½	cups sugar
1 tablespoon	baking powder
1 teaspoon	baking soda
3	eggs, well beaten
½ pint	sour cream
1 teaspoon	vanilla and/or other extracts to taste
½ cup	butter, melted and cooled
1 teaspoon	cocoa

Sift flour, sugar, baking powder and soda. Add eggs which have been beaten again with sour cream, vanilla or other extracts, and butter.

Knead dough and make into a ball. Divide into 4 pieces. Take each piece and roll out about 1 inch larger than pie plate. Put dough into buttered and floured 9-inch pie plate and let overhang. Put in ¼ of the filling. At one point make a diagonal cut of overhanging dough. Roll over the cut portion and make another diagonal cut, continue completely around pan.

Sprinkle top of filling with 1 teaspoon of powdered cocoa.

Bake at 350 degrees for 1 hour.

Delicatessen in Lucca

Zabaglione (Egg Custard with Marsala)

Zabaglione may be served hot or chilled, alone as a dessert or in combination with fruits or cake. It can be used as a festive topping for canned or fresh pear or peach halves, and is very delicious when served atop slices of sponge cake. If made with unflavored gelatin it can be placed in cups in freezer section and used as an iced cream.

Another attractive way of serving it is to arrange 3 or 4 lady finger halves in sherbet glasses and pour in the Zabaglione. It is neither very sweet nor very rich and for this reason makes a perfect finale for an otherwise hearty meal.

There is a very famous cake in San Francisco's North Beach which is made by placing Zabaglione in between layers of cake and then topping the entire cake with whipped cream and freezing it. The cake is called a Sacrapantina and the perfect version is available at Franco Santucci's Stella Pastry at Columbus and Green Streets.

3	egg yolks
½ cup	sugar
½ cup	sherry wine, marsala or madeira
1	lemon, grated rind and juice

Beat egg yolks slightly in upper part of cold double boiler. Add remaining ingredients, place over boiling water, and beat constantly with rotary egg beater or electric mixer until mixture thickens and fluffs up like whipped cream. Remove from heat and serve hot or chilled in sherbet glasses or spread on cakes.

Zabaglione Budino (Egg Pudding with Marsala)

In order to make Zabaglione Budino add

1 tablespoon	**cornstarch, sifted**
2 tablespoons	**flour, sifted**

to Zabaglione while beating with rotary egg beater or electric mixer over boiling water. Allow to cool.

NON SI FA COSA IN TERRA,
CHE PRIMA NON SIA SCRITTA IN CIELO
We do nothing on earth
that hasn't been written in Heaven

Miscellaneo

Miscellaneous

Verdura

(Vegetables)

One of the gates in the wall of Lucca

Carciofi
(Braised Artichokes)

1 pound small	artichokes
1	lemon, juiced
1	onion, quartered
to taste	salt and pepper
1 teaspoon	dried marjoram
½ teaspoon	garlic powder
approximately	
1 cup	chicken broth

Take off the outer leaves of artichokes, continuing until you reach the more tender leaves (about 2 or 3 layers). Then cut artichoke in half. Soak artichokes in cold water to which you have added lemon juice. Soak for 10 minutes. Arrange in a pan with quartered onions in the center. Salt and pepper and add marjoram and garlic powder. Cover artichokes half way up with chicken broth, either your own or from a can. Cover, lower flame, and cook about 20 minutes or until artichokes are tender.

Fiori di Zucchini (Zucchini Flowers)

4	zucchini blossoms
1	egg, well beaten
1 tablespoon	water
½ cup	flour
to taste	salt and pepper
¼ cup	vegetable oil
2 tablespoons	butter

Split zucchini blossoms down middle on one side, remove green flower end. Wash gently. Drain flower on paper toweling then dip in egg batter. Sprinkle with salt and pepper and when oil and butter are medium hot, place flower in pan gently. Fry for 1 minute, turn and fry an additional 2 minutes.

Frittata di Spinaci
(Spinach Omelet)

3 tablespoons	olive oil
½ medium	onion, diced
½ cup	crisply cooked bacon, crumbled
10	eggs, slightly beaten
10 ounce box	frozen, chopped spinach, thawed and drained
1 small clove	garlic, minced
1 teaspoon	salt
¼ teaspoon	pepper
1 tablespoon	fresh parsley, chopped
⅓ cup	Parmesan cheese, grated

Heat oil in 10 inch heavy skillet with a heat resistant handle. Add onion and saute until tender and golden brown, approximately 5 minutes. In a large bowl, combine remaining ingredients except cheese and beat with a wire whisk or fork until well blended. Turn into skillet with onion. Cook over low heat, lifting from bottom with spatula as the eggs set.

Put in oven and broil until top is set. Sprinkle with Parmesan and return to broiler for 1 minute. Use spatula to loosen from pan and slide onto serving platter. Cut into pie sized wedges.

Melanzana (Eggplant with Basic Tomato Sauce)

2 large	eggplants
⅔ cup	olive oil
3 cups	Soffritto (Basic Tomato Sauce)
to taste	salt and pepper
1 pound	ricotta cheese
2	eggs, beaten
¼ cup	whipping cream
½ cup	Parmesan cheese, grated

Take eggplants, wash outside, peel, and dry. Take off leafy top. Slice in ¼ inch lengthwise slices. Fry over medium heat on both sides in hot olive oil. Put 1 layer in a glass baking dish. Put on top of this, 1 layer of Soffritto. Put another layer of eggplant on top, continue alternating with Soffritto sauce, sprinkling each layer with salt and pepper. Then take ricotta cheese and eggs, blend well, add whipping cream, mix well again and pour over eggplant. Sprinkle surface with Parmesan cheese. Bake in a 450 degree oven 10 minutes, reduce to 375 degrees and continue to cook for another 30 to 45 minutes or until top is a rich crusty brown.

Soffritto recipe see page 145.

Patate Rosse
(Red Potatoes)

12 small	**red potatoes**
½ cup	**olive oil**
2 cloves	**garlic, minced**
½ cup	**parsley, chopped**

Place whole potatoes in pan with olive oil in oven and when potatoes start cooking, sprinkle with garlic and parsley. Bake in 350 degree oven until tender, approximately 45 minutes.

Marjoram

Piselli al Prosciutto (Sweet Peas with Italian Ham)

½ cube	butter
1	onion, chopped
¼ pound	prosciutto, cut into cubes
2-10 ounce boxes	frozen peas
to taste	salt and pepper

Melt butter in pan, add chopped onion and prosciutto and saute until onion is limp.

Add frozen peas, salt, and pepper and simmer, stirring frequently, for 12 to 15 minutes. Cover until ready to serve.

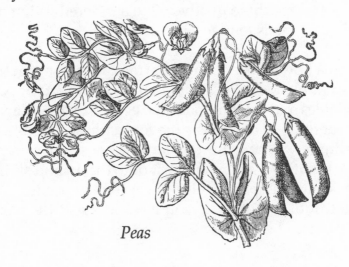

Peas

Zucchini Frittata (Zucchini Omelet)

If have your own garden and are lucky enough to have a zucchini plant, you'll understand why this recipe is called "the one that got away." Invariably one zucchino gets hidden away under all the leaves and by the time you find it, it's huge.

7 slices	salami, cut in strips
3	green onions, sliced including green tops
½	yellow onion, chopped
12	mushrooms, sliced
1 very large	zucchino, cubed
½ cup	olive oil
8	eggs, slightly beaten
1 cup	Parmesan cheese, grated

Saute salami slices, green onions, onion, mushrooms and zucchino in olive oil in a covered frying pan until zucchino is tender.

In a bowl mix eggs and Parmesan cheese together just until blended. Pour into pan and with a fork poke vegetables and salami under the eggs. Cover pan again and continue to cook over the lowest heat possible for 40 minutes. When the top looks almost set you can either flip it over by inverting it onto the lid and sliding it back into the pan or else place the pan under your broiler until top is set. If you have inverted the pan, 5 minutes will be sufficient.

Zucchini Torta (Zucchini Cake)

7	zucchini
8	eggs, slightly beaten
1 cup	Parmesan cheese, grated
3	green onions, chopped
¼ teaspoon	garlic powder
to taste	salt and pepper
7 slices	salami, cut in strips

Parboil zucchini. Drain water and mash zucchini lightly. Add all remaining ingredients, mix gently, and pour into a large greased baking dish. Bake for 45 minutes at 350 degrees.

Zucchini con Granchio (Crab Stuffed Zucchini)

4 medium	zucchini
2 tablepoons	butter
6	scallions, chopped
2 stalks	celery, chopped
2 large	carrots, shredded
2-6 ounce cans	crab meat, rinsed and drained
½ cup	seasoned dry bread crumbs
2 tablespoons	mayonnaise
4 teaspoons	lemon juice
4 slices	Swiss cheese, each cut into thin strips

Cut zucchini lengthwise in half. Cook uncovered in microwave on HIGH for 3 minutes. With spoon remove pulp, leaving a ¼ inch shell. Chop pulp, set aside.

In a frying pan, combine butter, scallions, celery and carrots. Stir in crab meat, bread crumbs, mayonnaise, lemon juice and reserved zucchini pulp. Place zucchini shells in a shallow baking dish. Divide crab mixture into eight equal portions, fill, and cover with vented plastic wrap. Cook on HIGH another 3 minutes, drain if required. Top with strips of cheese. Cook on HIGH another 2 to 3 minutes until heated through and cheese is melted.

Pane

(Breads)

Giovannini Bakery in Montecatini, the Tuscan town of spas, where Princess Marcella Borghese discoverd the formula for her "Terme di Montecatini" line of cosmetics.

Focaccia
(Italian Bread)

1-½ ounce package	yeast
1 cup	warm water
2 teaspoons	sugar
1 teaspoon	salt
¼ cup	olive oil
3 cups	flour
1-8 ounce can	chunky tomato sauce
1 tablespoon	oregano, chopped

In a very large bowl, dissolve yeast in water. Add sugar and wait until foamy, 5 or 10 minutes. Add salt and oil. Stir in the first 2 cups of flour. Use a mixer with a dough hook to knead dough until elastic, adding remaining flour as needed. Knead by hand a few minutes more, working in additional flour if necessary. Form into a ball. Place in a greased bowl. Turn to grease top of dough. Cover with a towel and let rise until double, about 1 hour. Punch down and knead again. Flatten dough into a large pizza pan or rectangular baking pan with shallow sides which has been lightly oiled. Punch holes with 2 fingers all over the dough. Top with your favorite chunky tomato sauce and sprinkle with oregano. Let rise once more. Bake at 450 degrees for 12 to 15 minutes. While hot dribble with additional olive oil and then cut into squares.

The other option and the one we like best is to put soaked raisins on top of dough and punch each one down with the 2 fingers and then sprinkle top with sugar.

Cooking grapes

Focaccina di Salsicce
(Spicy Sausage Muffins)

2 links	sweet Italian sausages, casings removed and broken into pieces
2 cups	flour
⅓ cup	Parmesan cheese, grated
1 tablespoon	baking powder
½ teaspoon	salt
⅛ teaspoon	black pepper, freshly ground
½ teaspoon	oregano, dried
1 large	egg
1-14 ounce jar	pizza sauce
2 tablespoons	olive oil

Place sausage meat in a skillet. Fry over moderate heat, stirring and breaking up sausage with a spoon until cooked and browned. Heat oven to 400 degrees.

Grease muffin cups or use foil or paper baking cups. Drain sausage on a paper towel—save fat in skillet. Thoroughly mix flour, Parmesan cheese, baking powder, salt, and pepper in a large bowl. Crumble the oregano in your fingers to release the flavor and stir into flour mixture and set aside. Break egg into a medium size bowl. Lightly beat with a fork or whisk, blending in pizza sauce. Add 3 tablespoons fat to sauce mixture, starting with sausage fat from skillet and making up the difference with olive oil as needed. Add sausage and mix well.

Pour sauce mixture over dry ingredients and mix gently until moistened. Scoop the very thick batter into muffin cups. Bake 20 to 25 minutes or until firm on top. Turn out onto a rack and cool at least 30 minutes before serving.

Pepper

Grissini
(Italian Bread Sticks)

1-¼ ounce package	yeast
⅓ cup	lukewarm water
2 tablespoons	salad oil
2 tablespoons	olive oil
1 teaspoon	salt
1 tablespoon	sugar
2¼ cups	flour
1	egg, well beaten
½ cup	sesame seeds

Dissolve yeast in the lukewarm water. Add the oils, salt, sugar, and 1 cup of flour. Mix until smooth. Add remaining flour and mix and knead until smooth and elastic. Place dough in a buttered bowl. Cover with a damp towel and let rise until doubled in size, about 1 hour. Punch dough down. Divide dough in half. Cut each half into 24 parts. Roll each part using palms of your hands until 6 or 8 inches long. Place parallel on a greased baking sheet, about ½ inch apart. Let rise in a warm place until doubled in size, about 30 minutes. Pat with sesame seeds and bake at 325 degrees for about 40 minutes or until golden brown.

Pane di Polenta (Polenta Bread)

1 cup	flour, sifted
1 cup	polenta
3 teaspoons	baking powder
½ teaspoon	salt
½ cup	sugar
1	egg, beaten
1 cup	milk
¼ cup	vegetable oil

Preheat oven to 425 degrees. Place all ingredients in mixing bowl and blend. Pour into 8 inch square greased pan and bake 20-25 minutes or until brown. May also be baked in muffin tins, greased or paper lined.

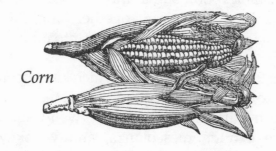

Corn

Panettone (Sweet Bread)

1 cup plus 1 tablespoon	sugar
2-1 ounce cakes	compressed yeast
2 cups	milk, scalded, cooled slightly
3 tablespoons	shortening
3	eggs, well beaten
4 cups	flour
1 teaspoon	salt
1 cup	raisins
1 cup	candied fruit
1 cup	pine nuts
½ teaspoon	anise extract
1 shot	mescolanza
1 shot	whiskey
½ cup	powdered sugar

Add 1 tablespoon sugar and compressed yeast to milk and mix well. Cream together shortening and remaining sugar. Add 2 eggs and stir into milk mixture.

Mix in 3 cups flour and salt which have been sifted together. Cover and let rise until doubled, about 1½ hours. Stir in raisins, candied fruit, well-floured pine nuts, anise extract, mescolanza, and whiskey. Add enough remaining flour to make a soft dough.

Knead until smooth and satiny. Form into 3 balls. Place on a greased cookie sheet and brush with 1 egg mixed with 1 tablespoon cold water. Let rise again to double. Bake at 350 degrees for 1 hour and 10 minutes. When removed from oven sprinkle lightly with powdered sugar while still hot.

NOTE: Mescolanza is an Italian liqueur which can be bought in Italian Delicatessens.

CHI SOFFIA NELLA POLVERE,
SE N'EMPIE GLI OCCHI
Who blows in the dust, fills his eyes with dust

My father's family homes, Ponte Della Madalena
Borgo a Mozzano, Lucca, Italy on the Via Del Breno on the
way to the Abetone ski resorts in the Garfagnana region.
Corsagna is located on top of the hill to the right.

Erbette e Spezie
(Herbs and Spices)

The following is a list of herbs and spices with a short explanation of their characteristics and common use.

Tastes vary, so experiment. For example, we always include borrage in our ravioli filling but some people don't care for it. We make our Pesto from basil but some may not care for the taste. I love rosemary on my chicken and steak but other members of our family don't care for it. Again, vary your recipes until you discover your favorites.

Even though there are many more herbs and spices, the spices I use most often and the herbs I have available year-round in my garden are the following:

ANISE (Anice): Anise grows from 18 inches upward. The leaves start out fairly large and then become feather-like. This feather-like herb was originally referred to as Pimpinella. The leaves eventually turn into gray-brown seeds which are cultivated by placing them on paper towels or cloth in the sun to dry. They may also be placed in an unlit oven for two days then placed in tightly sealed small jars. The taste is sweet and licorice-like and they are used to flavor cakes, soups, beverage, cookies, panettone, beef, and veal stews. It attracts mice.

BORAGE (Borragnine): Borage derives its name from coragio (courage) and borra (flock of wool). It is a beautiful plant which self-seeds and grows year round. It grows tall with pretty blue flowers. It attracts bees. As a tea it has been used for centuries to clear mucous from the throat. It is used in salads and tastes similar to cucumbers. The leaves may be boiled and used in place of spinach. We boil a fistful and add it to the filling for ravioli and sometimes use a small amount when making spaghetti sauces.

BASIL (Basilico): Basil will grow in the garden from spring until fall. Basil has either been loved or vilified. The early Romans believed that basil would only grow profusely if it was planted amid shouts and curses. When the French want to call a person raving mad, they say he is sowing the basil *(semer le basilic)*. Taken any way you might, the Italians love basil and feel that a home or garden where basil grows is well protected. In Italy a young man usually offers a girl he loves a sprig of basil and if she in turn puts a pot of basil on the balcony or by a window it usually means she accepts his offer of marriage.

The tops are pinched so that the bush becomes wider and heartier and pickings are usually pinched every two or three weeks. The clove-like flavor is an asset in soups, salad dressings, egg dishes, and, of course, pesto. One of our favorite sandwiches is chopped basil mixed with sweet butter and spread on bread. As a tea it supposedly helps rheumatism.

BAY (Alloro): Bay grows rapidly into a large bush or tree. The bay leaves are very powerful and usually one leaf suffices in any recipe. The leaves can be picked and dried year round and they are becoming increasingly popular when formed into wreaths and given as gifts for Thanksgiving and Christmas. The leaves put into corner areas are a deterrent for fleas. The fleas hate them and run away from them. If placed in canisters, they will prevent bugs in flour and cereals. Bay leaves are used for sores and may be applied on wounds.

CAMOMILE (Camomilla): My mother-in-law swears by camomile. Whenever my husband was nervous or the boys had colic, were cranky, or were having nightmares, her remedy was camomile. The Romans used the tea for toothaches and the blonde women of Italy have used it as a hair rinse for centuries. I can't seem to grow it in our yard but some friends of ours, Italia and Dominic Brattesani, have it growing profusely in their yard, which is only a few short blocks from where we live in San Francisco.

Camomile is useful as a tonic. It is usually brewed as a tea, one ounce to a pint of boiling water.

The seeds are usually sown in lightly packed soil in August of each year and by early September the plants will have developed. Plants are extremely hardy. When developed, the seeds are picked, dried, and placed in tightly covered jars.

CHIVES (Erba Cipollina): Chives grow in clumps and the tender spears are usually cut into segments and are delicious when sprinkled on baked potatoes with sour cream. When cut into segments they can be dried in an unlit oven and then packed in freezer storage bags in the freezer. Chives are said to aid the digestion of fat.

CINNAMON (Cannella): Sweet, spicy. Used in baking.

CLOVES (Chiodo di Garofano): Sharp, spicy. Used with ham, other pork dishes, and cakes. May be burned in rooms to eliminate cooking odors.

FENNEL (Finocchio): Fennel must be started from seeds. Fennel, however, has a harmful effect on bush beans and tomatoes and must be planted away from them. The Romans believe that fennel tea was good for pregnant women and as a tea it is used to prevent colic. The leaves are used in salads, stews, and vegetables, with boiled fish, and the stalks are used to skewer cubes of pork for barbecuing.

MARJORAM (Maggiorana): Sweet Marjoram is the most popular with Italian gardeners in the United States. Unlike most herbs it retains its full flavor when dried. In the kitchen it is used with green vegetables, turkey, pork, lamb and eggs. Medicinally it is used to prevent colds, headaches, and nervousness. Steep 1 teaspoonful in a cup of hot water for about 10 minutes.

MINT (Menta): Mint was first used to deodorize homes and for bathwater. It is seldom used in Italian cooking but is used more as a tea for stomach ache. As a tea it is used in Europe to stimulate appetite and as an aphrodisiac for cramps and muscle spasms, and as a remedy for colds and flu.

Yerba Buena, as it is referred to in Italy, is easily cultivated and adds fragrance to the herb garden. It is mostly used in Italy to flavor liqueurs.

NUTMEG (Noce Moscata): Sweet, distinctive. Whole nuts which are grated and used in veal dishes but may be used sparingly in all meat dishes and in most baking. This is the spice most preferred in Northern Italian cooking.

OREGANO: Oregano can be planted from seed or cuttings. It requires little water and rainfall is usually sufficient. As soon as flowers appear, it is ready for harvest but may be picked for fresh use continually. Cutting off the tops and leaving one inch growth usually stimulates bushy growths. It is used profusely in Southern Italy but in Northern Italy it is used sparingly usually in combination with other herbs. It is used on pizza, in spaghetti sauces and other tomato dishes. If you like its flavor it can also be used in beef or lamb stews, salads and in tomato juice.

PARSLEY (Prezzemolo): Yes, it is a herb. It was intertwined in the crowns of the olympic victors. The Italians believe that a fine harvest of parsley is assured only when it is planted on Good Friday. Parsley is used in America mainly as a garnish but, in Italy, a dish seldom leaves the kitchen without parsley having been cooked into it. In a garden it grows so slowly that legend has it that parsley has to go to the Devil and back seven times before it comes up. It is supposedly good for stomach ailments, to cure bites, and stings of insects.

ROSEMARY (Rosmarino): Rosemary ranks as the noblest of herbs. It is a symbol of fidelity and remembrance and in Italy is used in weddings and at funerals. On the wedding night, sprigs of rosemary are placed under the newlyweds' pillows. When visiting cemeteries, sprigs of rosemary are usually placed with the flowers especially during the Christmas season because in Italy it is associated with the Virgin Mary. As legend has it, Mary draped her blue cloak over a white flowering rosemary bush during the flight from Egypt and, ever after, the noble plant embraced the hue of the Virgin's cloak.

Usually only one to five of every ten seeds planted will germinate and it may take up to three years to produce a cutable bush from seed. It flourishes with occasional watering. It can be left outside year round but during cold weather must be protected. It prefers a sunny location.

Medicinally it strengthens the memory. It is a tangy herb and is used to flavor beef, veal, pork, lamb, poultry, soups, stuffings, and sauces.

SAGE (Salvia): Sage is associated with immortality and is used for headaches and sore throats. Its Italian name, *salvia*, means health or salvation. It produces purplish flowers which appear in August. The Arabs call it "camel's tongue" because of its stubbly silver hair. It should be pruned in spring. It is used in Italy to whiten teeth. It is profusely used with game dishes. It is considered too strong for turkey or chicken but, used sparingly on chicken, it gives a strange taste which is either loved or hated.

TARRAGON (Dragoncello): The Italian name means little dragon. It was thought to draw the venom from the bites of snakes, insects, and mad dogs.

In addition to being used for making tarragon vinegar it is usually used with fish, cheese, eggs and spinach, peas, and lima beans.

It will grow to two or three feet and will have long leaves and yellow flowers in August. Harvest it in July when the lower leaves start to turn yellow.

THYME (Timo): Thyme attracts bees. In Italy it is planted as cover under fruit trees to attract pollinating bees. Traditionally it was placed in Christ's manger and is a favored plant in the gardens of churches and the California missions.

In Italy it is used as freely as salt in practically every dish: red meat, poultry, fish, and vegetables. For harvesting, the long stems are cut one inch off the ground and laid in the sun to dry. The leaves are removed, placed in freezer bags or glass jars, and enjoyed the entire year.

VARIETY: Take 1 large bay leaf, 1 sprig of thyme, 8 sprigs of fresh parsley, put in some cloth, tie, then throw in pot.

Of course, this list is not all the herbs available or used but is merely a list of those planted in our San Francisco Italian-American garden.

Sage

I DENARI NON BASTANO,
BISOGNA SAPERLI SPENDERE
Money is not enough,
we have to know how to spend it

Caffé Italiano
(Italian Coffee)

---

3 cups	strong black coffee
6 tablespoons	molasses
1 cup	heavy cream, whipped
	grated nutmeg

Mix coffee and molasses, stirring until dissolved. Heat to very hot. Divide evenly in 6 coffee glasses. Top each cup with whipped cream and sprinkle cream with grated nutmeg.

Add amaretto liqueur to taste by dripping in drops.

Sip coffee through the cream. Do not stir.

San Francisco coffee houses all located within a 5 block radius: Caffe Freddy's, Caffe Greco, Caffe Italia, Caffe Malvina, Caffe Puccini, Caffe Roma, Caffe Sport, Caffe Trieste.

Formaggio Parmigiano (Parmesan Cheese)

Parmesan cheese so often used in Tuscan cooking comes to us by way of the city of Parma which is east of Bologna in the Emilia Romagna region of Italy. The ancient formula has remained unchanged for 700 years. 60,000 farmers a day supply milk for 1,500 cheese-makers. About 4,000 to 10,000 cheese rounds are produced each day. The cows whose milk is used in the production of Parmesan cheese are placed on a special diet.

Parmesan cheese

Pancetta (Italian Bacon)

Italian cooks use pancetta in dishes such as sauces, stews, and soups. Pancetta is unsmoked, peppered bacon. It is purchased in thin rounds or as a flat slab of seasoned pork belly, that is rolled into a thick sausage shape. It is available in Italian delicatessens. When purchased in rounds it can be unwound into bacon like strips. Pancetta will keep in the refrigerator for three weeks or in the freezer for up to three months.

Pancetta is made on farms throughout Tuscany. Flat slabs of pork belly are rubbed with salt. After 48 hours a paste of pepper, saltpeter, sugar, and water which has boiled 15 minutes is spread on top with a heavy weight to keep it under the brine. It will keep like this about a year, or after 5 weeks it can be rolled, tied and hung to dry. When dry it is usually smoked.

Prosciutto (Italian Ham)

EMIGLIA ROMAGNA that borders Tuscany on the northeast, is the home of both Parmigiano Cheese (from the City of Parma) and prosciutto (Italian Ham). The prosciutto which is so often used in the recipes of this book, is mainly cured in this region of Italy. The climate, the quality of the hind legs of pork and the purity of the spring waters all add to making the most superior ham product in all of Italy. Throughout the region, during the drying season, prosciutto hangs from the ceilings of all the buildings. It is usually cured with the onset of cooler weather, temperatures being ideal between 50 to 60 degrees Fahrenheit. After the legs are trimmed to shape, they are cured with salt, sugar, peppercorns and saltpeter. The flesh is allowed to absorb the salt mixture and the legs remain hanging from 7 to 8 weeks. The hams are turned once a week for the entire hanging time. The mold is then removed with stiff brushing and the hams are covered with a new mixture of fresh pork fat, flour, salt, pepper and water, thus sealing the hams. They are then rehung at 50 to 60 degree temperature for an additional 24 weeks. In all, the hams are usually cured for at least 8 to 10 months. Local farmers say that the special flavor of Parma Hams is derived from the aging under the above conditions.

A FAR DEL BENE A GLI IGNORANTI
SE NA PER MALE DIO E I SANTI
To do good to the ignorant
would upset God and the Saints

During the 15 years I worked in San Francisco's movie industry, WOMPI (Women of the Motion Picture Industry) compiled a cookbook. I have taken the liberty of reprinting the following pages as a "thank you" for the memories.

Anna Maria Alberghetti
Alan Alda
Michelangelo Antonioni
Armand Assante
Frankie Avalon

John Belushi
Tony Bennett
Bernardo Bertolucci
Joseph Bologna
Sony Bono
Marlon Brando
Rossano Brazzi
Argentina Brunetti
Victor Buono

Gianna Maria Canale
Judy Canova
Frank Capra
Claudia Cardinale
Nicola Carraro
John Cassavetes
Tony Charmoli
Lewis Ciannelli
Michael Cimino
Perry Como
John Conte
Francis Ford Coppola
Vanentina Cortese
Franco Cristaldi

Vic Damone
Beverly D'Angelo
Dino De Laurentis
Robert De Niro
Johnny Desmond

Aldo Fabrizi
James Farentino
Fabian Forte
Anthony Franciosa

Vincent Gardenia
Vittorio Gassman
Giancarlo Giannini
Harry Guardino

Jake La Motta
    "The Raging Bull"
Mario Lanza
Gina Lollobrigida
Sophia Loren

Nino Manfredi
Silvanna Mangano
Marcello Mastroianni
Liza Minelli
Rocky and Lou Marciano
Dean Martin
Tony Musante

Ramon Navarro
Franco Nero

Al Pacino
Silvanna Pampanini
Pier Paolo Pasolini
Luciano Pavarotti
Rosanna Podesta
Carlo Ponti

Aldo Ray

Albert Salmi
Susan Sarandon
Isabella Rossellini Scorsese
Martin Scorsese
Talia Shire
Frank Sinatra
Paul Sorvino
Sylvester Stallone

Ugo Tognazzi
Mel Torme
Daniel J. Travanti
John Travolta

Brenda Vaccaro
Jack Valenti
Rudolph Valentino
Alida Valli
Raf Vallone
Joseph Vitale
Milly Vitale
Monica Vitti
Gian Maria Volonte

Franco Zeffirelli

Works Consulted

Food, Waverly Root (Simon and Schuster, 1980).

Herbs for the Kitchen, Irma Goodrich Mazza (Little, Brown & Co., 1943).

Accent on Seasoning, Irma Goodrich Mazza (Little, Brown & Co., 1956).

Acknowledgments

Cheesecake with Almonds—Judy Taylor Kimball, Editor

Curing Green Olives—Dino Ferrari

Penne Arabiate and *Pasta Al Limone*—Caesar's Restaurant, John Brattesani

Red Snapper with Pancetta—Waterfront Cafe, Pier 7, S.F., Dan Falacchi

Salsa per Spaghetti—Dino Ferrari

Sausages—Marianno Barsotti, Roseville, CA.

Stuffed Mushroom Caps—Anna Figone, wife of Judge Richard Figone, mother of Cristina and Nicolas Figone.

Special "Grazie"

With sincere gratitude and a wish for good days and good food always.

Editor: Judy Taylor Kimball who deserves special appreciation for devoting hours of precious time checking accuracy and consistency, and for her good taste in everything.

Photographers:
Photo Links, San Francisco (Kit Haskel, Proprietor)
Domenico Tanni, *Il Tirreno* (Tuscan newspaper), Lucca, Italy
Joseph Enrico Figone, Corsagna, 1991

Translators:
Paola Bagnatori (Museo Italo-Americano, S.F.)
Maria Barsotti Della Santina, San Rafael
Romano Della Santina, Marin Joe's, Corte Madera

Thanks to Nancy and Paul Clemens who became not only the publishers but friends through an instant comradery. And to Linda Maxwell at Blue Dolphin for correcting and refining the entire text.

Gloria Romano, to whose son this book was dedicated, and Liana G. Figone, the author

Italian Index

MISCELLANEO (Miscellaneous)

Verdure (Vegetables)

Pane (Breads)

Carne (Meats)

English Index